AF429762

# Universal Truth:
## What the Buddha Really Taught

## Bryan Malakou

# About the Author

Dr. Bryan Malakou was born in Johannesburg South Africa. He is an ENT Surgeon in private practice. He was raised as a Roman Catholic and became a serious spiritual seeker in his early 20s, but feels he did not find his real path until about 10 years ago. It began with reading the works of Eckhart Tolle, which lead to studying Buddhism, Tao Te Ching by Laozi, the Greek Stoics, the Upanishads, Bhagavad Gita and other Yogi teachings notably made clear by Michael Singer, a Course in Miracles, and then full circle back to the teachings of Jesus. This lead to a direct realization of Universal Truth, which was gradual and slow, and is ongoing and incomplete.

After spending some time studying Buddhism he realized that all true spiritual teaching points in the same direction. The Buddha was a fully enlightened being who had the wonderful gift of being a superb teacher. He spoon-feeds us with a didactic step by step process, which leads to the end of suffering and awakening. He makes the point though, that neither he nor anyone else, can do it for you. He can give you an outline of how to do it, but you have to seek, make the right effort, and realize the truth yourself.

# Contents

# Forward

Humans exist in a state of dukkha, which means suffering or unsatisfactoriness. External things in the world, are not able to overcome this state for any length of time. The Buddha shows the way to the end of suffering, which is permanent. It is possible to live your life in perfect peace and joy. You can see the world through new eyes, and this recreates the world that you live in.

The Buddha tells us how we can do this. He points the way, but the responsibility to practice it and realize the truth is up to the individual. This book outlines the basics of what the Buddha taught. It is not meant to be a comprehensive collection of the vast teachings found in Buddhist literature. Use it as a springboard to learn and implement the basic teachings of the Buddha. It is the beginning of an exciting journey.

I have tried to stick to the original teachings that the Buddha himself taught, and not delve into the teachings that developed hundreds of years later. I have used some Pali terms and if the Sanskrit term is better known, I have used that, but I have kept it to a minimum. These are wonderful spiritually descriptive languages, which in one word conveys what takes half a page in English

# Chapter 1

# History of Buddhism

Many religions including Buddhism, started with core universal truth teachings. With time and input from many of their followers, the message often gets distorted. The simple truth becomes complicated and often gets hidden beneath dogma, and ritual gradually builds up around these truths. The teachings that once were alive, vibrant, and life-changing become confusing and often empty. Buddhism is no exception.

The Buddha was born into the family of the Shakaya clan in northern India arguably in the year 563 BC. He was known as Prince Siddharta Gautama and was destined to take over as king of the clan, but on observing extensive suffering and dissatisfaction among all people, at the age of 29, he renounced his inheritance. He set out to find a way to overcome suffering in the world.

Six years later at the age of 35 under the famous Bodhi tree in Bodh Gaya northern India, he attained enlightenment or awakening. From then on he was known as Shakayamina Buddha, which means "the awakened sage of the Shakya clan". He spent the next 45 years of his life wandering around teaching anyone interested in these universal truths that had been revealed to him. He died at the age of 80 in 483 BC although there is some doubt about the exact dates of his birth and death.

The Buddha had experienced a life of luxury and plenty, and when he started his search for truth, he at first went completely the other way. He became an ascetic depriving himself of many of life's pleasures. He hardly ate, wasted away until he became weak, withered and shrunken.

One day he took stock of himself and realized he could not think clearly, and that he was further away from his goal than when he first started. It is said he went for a swim and nearly drowned and as he lay on the river bank recovering, he realized that, if he was going to succeed, he would have to follow the middle way. The middle way is a path between self-indulgence and extreme self-denial. This middle way has taken on more meaning in Buddhism and is widely known as the way that avoids all extremes.

After his Enlightenment, the Buddha traveled around teaching what is known as the dharma, which is about the law of the cause of suffering and the path to the cessation of suffering. Many teachings in Buddhism are taught in the negative. Thus, Christians might call the same thing, attaining a peace that passes all understanding, the Buddha taught overcoming suffering, but in fact, it is one and the same.

When the Buddha died one of his foremost disciples convened a meeting and gathered 500 of his most respected disciples. At this meeting, someone who had heard a teaching would relate exactly what was taught, and this had to be verified by others who had been there, and once the exact teaching was established the 500 were told to commit the teaching to memory. The teachings were divided into three baskets known as the Tripitaka in Sanskrit, when they were finally written down, some 400 years after the Buddha's death.

**The basket of discourses**: which contained the clarification to the path that leads to the end of suffering.

**The basket of discipline:** this was for monks and nuns and the Buddha had formulated these as problems arose. These rules apply mainly to those who chose the monastic way of life and developed over time as they were needed.

**The basket of higher teachings**: the Buddha often emphasized that it was fruitless to indulge in philosophical speculation. Dwelling on questions like "does the world have a beginning and an end?" is of little value. These teachings outline how ignorance perpetuates suffering and related philosophical teachings.

The second Council meeting occurred about 60 years later by this time there were many disagreements on the spirit of the Buddha's teachings and the first split into two groups occurred. Although over time many more splits and divisions have occurred these two groups are still recognizable.

**Therevada** –Doctrine of the Elders-- is practiced primarily in Sri Lanka, Southeast Asian countries such as Myanmar and Thailand.

**Mahayana** –The Great Vehicle is practiced in Nepal, Tibet, Mongolia, Taiwan, China, and Japan. Tibetan Buddhism headed by the Dala Lama originated from this branch(now called **Vajrayana**).

The point is that Buddha's teachings were handed down orally for 400 years in various languages and dialects and only in the first century BC was the Pali Canon written down in Sri Lanka. I am not going to discuss the merits of the many different traditions and forms of Buddhism that exist today. It is however safe to say, that many rituals and human-made dogmas have crept in, which serves to muddy the waters, and obscure the simple core teachings of the Universal Truths that the Buddha taught.

I am not a committed Buddhist or a scholar of Buddhism. I am a learner and teacher of Universal Truth wherever it comes from. This book seeks to cut through the confusion and attempts to clarify the core teachings of the Buddha. The purpose of these teachings is to lead you to the end of suffering and Nirvana, or Christian speak, to peace of mind and joy which is the Kingdom of Heaven within. These are the same thing.

There are many books on the development and spread of the different traditions of Buddhism. The main divisions today are Theravada, Mahayana (the Great Vehicle) Hinayana (the lesser vehicle), Vajrayana (Tantric), and Zen (Chan in China) Buddhism.

In this book, I am not going to concern myself with the different traditions which have different emphases. It is safe to say that they all have the goal of finding a path to the end of suffering and reaching Nirvana, which is a state of joy.

Many traditions and rituals have built up intending to help people to achieve this. They may be helpful to some people and not helpful to others. None of them are essential. There are many different paths to awakening aimed at reaching the top of the mountain so to speak. Meditation of some sort is essential in all forms of Buddhism to know the Universal Truth.

In some traditions, there are ritualistic mudras like committing to doing 100,000 prostrations. There are mantras, meditation techniques, prayer wheels, and other ritualistic techniques. These can all be helpful but the danger is that they can become an end in themselves. They may help to purify and concentrate the mind and overcome defilements, but it is important to always be aware of the end goal which we will discuss in detail in this book.

By all means, use the many Buddhist techniques out there to help reach non—dualism, but don't fall into the trap of making these techniques an end in itself.

Another thing that is often taught that I don't believe is true is that awakening is extremely rare and only happens to a few individuals every one thousand years or so, or that maybe when you have reincarnated another 1000 times you may achieve it. This makes out that awakening is so difficult, that it is for practical purposes unachievable for most people.

I do not believe this is true. It is achievable. It is easy but not simple. Seek and ye shall find! All you can do is prepare the way. Knock and the door will be opened, and keep knocking until it is opened. The final step, I believe comes as a grace-a gift from the universe if you like. There are however many benefits to be had along the journey until you get there and when you get there it is an ongoing, never-ending, evolving process. It is not a goal you reach, it is a state of being in the present moment. If it is made into a concept then that is not it.

In the time of the Buddha, India had a strong caste system but the Buddha did not discriminate and taught people who were willing to hear his message, from the lowest to the highest castes. At the top of the heap were the Brahmins or priests but the Buddha taught that the true Brahmins were people of high moral character.
As he said, " He who is tolerant to the intolerant, peaceful to the violent, who is free from greed, who speaks words that are calm, helpful, and true, and that offends no-one: him I call a Brahmin."
He would teach both sexes and all ages, adapting his teaching to the people he was speaking to. He even allowed, after some hesitation, his female followers to become nuns and enter monasteries. This was not an

acceptable practice at that time and there was much resistance to this.

# Chapter 2

# The Four Noble Truths and Eightfold Noble Path

Siddhartha had crossed the river and made his way to a large fig tree known as the Bodhi tree, determined not to leave until he reached enlightenment.

The Buddha entered deep meditation. He did struggle with doubts and mental demons, but eventually at a full moon on the night of his Enlightenment he gradually penetrated truth and passed through different stages of deep meditation. "The fires of his growing wisdom burned away whatever level of unknowing still obscured his mind. He gradually penetrated subtler levels of ignorance. He clearly saw how craving, the source of suffering, is rooted in ignorance. As the sun came up he said he achieved complete enlightenment.

For seven weeks the Buddha stayed in the region of the Bodhi tree, absorbed in the limitless bliss of awareness. At first, he thought no one else could understand or enjoy the fruits of his enlightenment and he kept it to himself. He soon realized that some people could benefit from his teachings. His concern was that people would be unable to grasp the depth of his teaching.

When he had been in the forest there had been five ascetics there with him. They had been disappointed when he left that way of life for the middle way. They thought he was a quitter. He sought them out and found them at the Deer Park in Sarnath. At first, they were resistant, but they could not help notice that a profound change had come over him. He radiated peaceful assurance and benevolence, and they welcomed him with respect, asking him to reveal his experience.

He then gave his first discourse or sutta as the Buddhists now call it. This was the first turning of the wheel. The Buddha made it clear to them that he could not remove suffering from others like removing a thorn, but he could teach them the path of doing it themselves. No-one else can do it for you, you need to be still, meditate and seek experiential inner knowledge or wisdom. The Buddha was later known for tailoring his teaching to individuals, by teaching what is best suited to that person's make-up. Not every teaching was verbal as he could provide spiritual inspiration and instruction by his presence, and convey deep meaning in silence.

### The Four Noble Truths

This was known as the first turning of the wheel, or the first sutta, which he gave at Deer Park in Sarnath. In English, we call it his first discourse or teaching.

1. Dukkha exists (suffering exists)
2. The cause of dukkha is craving or desire.
3. Dukkha can be overcome by removing the craving
4. The path to doing this is the Noble Eight-fold Path.


**1. Dukkha exists**: Dukkha is a Pali word which has no direct translation into English. It means suffering, but the meaning is far broader than this. The ancient Aryans brought the Sanskrit language to India. They were a tribe that kept cattle and oxen which pulled their carriages. Dukkha originally meant "bumpy axle" or "rough ride". In Sanskrit, it came to mean suffering or dissatisfaction. It is used to describe the full range from overt suffering to just a feeling of underlying anxiety or uneasiness. It could mean a feeling that something is missing, that there must be something out there that might fulfill you. Dukkha covers everything in human existence that is not love and joy.

Certain experiences in life are so painful and miserable that no one has any difficulty in identifying them as suffering. Acute physical discomfort or pain might fall into that category. In his discourse, the Buddha specifically mentioned birth, death, and aging. He gave the examples of sickness, of not getting what you want and getting what you do not want. There may be short periods of bliss and joy but this is not a state of being most of the time.

The first noble truth said the Buddha is that human existence is one of dukkha or unsatisfactoriness.

**The cause of dukkha is craving**: The Buddha described how pervasive suffering is. It is a condition that almost all humans live with. The obvious next question is "What is the cause of this?" The  Buddha said that all dukkha comes from desirous attachment or craving and that this craving is caused by ignorance. If you scrutinize desire closely, you will see that it is intimately tied to dukkha and they are inseparable. Let us consider the cycle of desire. The moment it arises, it creates a sense of lack or want, and to bring this pain to an end we seek to fulfill the desire. If we fail it brings pain, frustration, or even despair. If we succeed we fear losing it. We then desire to safeguard our position and we worry that we may lose ground on our gain. We want what we have gained to last forever. All objects of desire are impermanent, whether it be wealth, power, position, or persons, separation is inevitable. The pain of this separation is proportional to the force of our attachment.

This egoic thought process is all-pervasive, because of ignorance. He meant ignorance about reality and about who we are and the nature of creation.


If you allow desires for this and that to lead you around by the nose, you will experience repeated dissatisfaction and you will never know true peace and satisfaction. Creation has been evolving for 13.8 billion years, and for most circumstances outside of us, we have limited control. Unless you learn to surrender to what is, to love what is, you will live in a state of continuous dukkha. The Buddha called giving up desire renunciation. Unless you learn to see the world through different eyes you are doomed to live in this state.

Most of us make our happiness conditional on what is happening outside of us. If I have a partner who behaves in a certain way, if I have good health, if I have enough money and so on, then only will I be happy. Most of us live for the future and we do not live in the present moment. When I achieve this or that when this or that happens then will I be happy. Almost always, when this or that is achieved, we move the goalposts, and there will be some other thing that we think we need. It becomes a vicious cycle and nothing permanently satisfies us.

It is insanity to live like this. When something we perceive as bad happens to us we resist it and we deny it. What ends up happening, is resistant thoughts about what happened become the source of our ongoing unhappiness.

That is to say, it is not what happened, it's our thoughts about what happened that is the source of our suffering. When things happen it is crazy to resist it. It has happened and it is a fact. Meet it head-on and accept it. You can change your thoughts to accept what is.

When someone attacks you verbally, your instinct is to defend yourself and attack back. You want to force the other person to behave in another way. You desire different behavior from the person, and try to force them to make that happen. You tell yourself "If I can do that then I will be happy". Know that the other person is doing the best they can, with their state of consciousness and wisdom at the time. Remove your desire that their behavior is different. Do not judge, and accept them as they are. That is how humans who are ignorant about the way to the end of suffering behave. Have sympathy as their ignorance leads to bad karma and future suffering.

Hollywood is a great teacher. If you think that being popular, rich, famous, good-looking, and sexually attractive to the opposite sex is the key to your happiness, think again. Many of these very people have all of this and more, and yet there is no evidence that they are happier than ordinary people. Lasting happiness is not gained by any of these things. Happiness comes from healing yourself inside, not trying to manipulate external conditions.

"The cause of dukkha is desire" needs to be clarified and qualified. To do that, let us look at the structure of the human mind as if it were concentric layers of a circle. The very inside of the circle drives and affects the function of the layers outside of it.

So right on the outside of the circle is (see Fig 1)

**Perception**-- which is how we perceive the world outside of us, with our five senses. For us, how we see the world outside of us is our reality.

**Emotional layer**-- for most of us in the world, this is actually a fear layer. Even what we call "love" in special relationships is fear-based. It is driven by a desire that people outside of us will behave in a certain way, which will make us happy. If they do not behave in a way that we want them to, this ephemeral happiness dissolves. This almost inevitably happens at some point in a relationship based on this kind of love. The layer beneath this drives our emotions.

**Thought layer**--- what we think, which includes our expectations and judgments of life events, determines what happens in our emotional layer.

**Belief layer**-- what we believe about how the world works or how it should be, will determine what faults we have.

**Desire layer**—right at the centre of the circle is desire which determines what happens through all the layers above us, culminating in how we perceive the world outside. Thus if our life is one of dukkha, we need to look at the very centre of the circle for the cause. If we can change the desire layer of our mind, all the layers above change. This will result in changing the way we perceive the world, and you could say we are creating our own "bubble world" which becomes true for us.

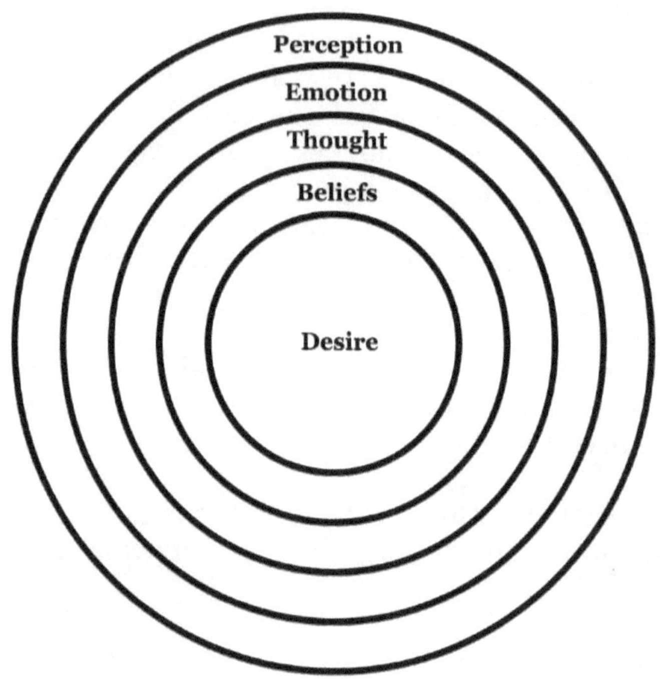


The Buddha said to **remove the desire to overcome suffering**. In truth, we need to replace the desire for things of the world with a desire for correct things.

What are these correct things that we should desire? These things are universal truths which means the reality of creation or non-delusion, the true nature of who we are. We need to desire the path that leads to the end of suffering. This is where we will discover that we are love. This is where the end of suffering (the Kingdom of Heaven or Nirvana) and the peace that passes all understanding will be found.

But let us tarry a little, I have jumped to the end but we are still taking the baby steps of the Buddha's very first sutta, where he gives us a broad outline of the path we need to take to awakening. This is the Fourth Noble Truth.

**The Noble Eightfold Path**

Right View
Right Intention
Right Speech
Right Action
Right Livelihood
Right Effort
Right Mindfulness
Right Concentration

This is the way to the end of suffering, the fourth noble truth. Let us look at what is meant by all these steps. These steps are more like components of a whole that are intertwined and inter-dependant. They all depend on each other and none can survive on their own because they are all parts of a whole. They are the eight spokes of the wheel, all of which are needed to allow the wheel to function properly, and allow the turning of the wheel. For practical training, the Noble Eightfold path can be divided into three groups. Panna→ Sila→Samadhi→Panna

Panna: The wisdom group, made up of the right view and right intention. It is both the beginning and the end of the path. We start with limited wisdom, perfect it by laying the foundation in the moral group, and then penetrating it in the concentration group and then this wisdom can lead us directly to awakening.

Sila: The moral discipline group: -right speech, right action, and right livelihood. It is worth repeating that moral discipline is the foundation of concentration, which is the foundation of wisdom, which is the direct instrument of liberation from suffering.

Samadhi: The concentration(or mental culture) group:-- right effort, right mindfulness, and right concentration

So although the right view (wisdom group) comes at the end, to start on the path we need at least a vague view of the right intention. It is the seed of the fruit and without the seed, the fruit cannot grow.

In truth, the wholeness of the right view encompasses understanding the entire Dharma (the entire teachings of the Buddha), but this is grasped in stages using the other members of the Noble Eightfold Path. The right view is both the beginning and the end. If for example, you were driving your car to a destination in another city, you would start in the general direction of the other city, by getting onto the highway that leads there. As you approach the city, you would use maps or a GPS to refine the road you would take to the exact address of the final destination. So too with the right view, do you need to start with some idea of the direction you are heading in.

Again, for the purposes of instruction, the Buddha divides the right view into two groups.

# 1. Right View
Mundane right view
Supermundane right view


## Mundane Right View

Karma (Sanskrit) Kamma(Pali)

The mundane right view requires at the outset that we have an understanding of the law of karma. Kamma ahata sammaditthi literally translated means "right view of the ownership of action". It is summed up in the following statement: "Beings are the owners of their actions, the heirs of their actions, they spring from their actions, are bound to their actions, and are supported by their actions. Whatever deeds they do, good or bad, of those they shall be heirs". In short, you could say "you reap what you sow".

Good karma, are actions that lead to the end of suffering and Nirvana. Bad karma, are actions that lead to suffering for yourself and others. The word karma means action, but Buddhism teaches that the relevant action is volitional action. This means that action needs to be willed and performed through body, speech, or mind. Karma is essentially a mental event expressed through the body as an action, through speech as verbal action, through thoughts as plans, ideas, or other mental states, without at that stage gaining outer expression. These three types of karmic action all have an element of volition in common.

The right view, not only recognizes that action has consequences or fruits, but it recognizes the difference between wholesome action and unwholesome action. A disciple needs to understand what is karmically wholesome, and the root of this, and what is karmically unwholesome and what the root of this is. Unwholesome karma is an action that is morally blameworthy, detrimental to spiritual development, and conducive to suffering for oneself and others. Wholesome action, on the other hand, is an action that is morally commendable, helpful to spiritual growth, and productive of benefits for oneself and others. Developing the skill to understand this fully, requires the development of wisdom.

Although **unwholesome actions** are innumerable, the Buddha cited 10, three of bodily, four of verbal, and three mental.

Destroying life
Taking what is not given
Wrong conduct concerning sense pleasures
False speech
Slanderous speech
Harsh speech
Idle chatter
Covetousness
Ill will
Wrong view

Wholesome karma, he said, is abstaining from the first seven and being free from the last three. Karmic actions are distinguished as wholesome or unwholesome based on the underlying motives called roots. For example, if soldiers of a cruel regime came looking for a fugitive hiding in your house and they asked you if you knew where the fugitive is. If you lie and say you have not seen him, the roots are wholesome and therefore the action is wholesome. Thus there is a subtle, yet important difference between right speech and do not lie! It is all about the intention behind the action.

There are three roots each for unwholesome or wholesome karmic action. **The three roots of unwholesome karmic action, sometimes called the three poisons, which lead to defilements are:**
1. Greed
2. Aversion (hate, anger)
3. Delusion (ignorance)
The three roots for wholesome karmic action are non-greed, non-aversion, and non-delusion. So in a word right view (or right understanding) is the absence of delusion (ignorance or misunderstanding), which leads to the absence of greed and aversion.

These three roots of greed, hate, and delusion are all intertwined. Put succinctly, greed drives us to cling to or hoard the things we want. The Buddha called this attachment.

Aversion drives us to avoid and resist what we do not want. Aversion includes hate, anger, resentment, and even depression. Anything you dislike, resist or push away from you is aversion.

Delusion is ignorance about what factors lead to the end of suffering, and what factors lead to dukkha.

Delusion is the folly of thinking we can get what we want and exclude what we do not want, and believing that will be the end of dukkha.

Delusion results in the failure to recognize, that greed and hate are two sides of the same coin. In other words, clinging to something that I want is resistance to something that I do not want. My resistance to something I do not want resides in my preference for something I do want. When you resist circumstances when you resist what is, you are certain to suffer. The tug-of-war between clinging and aversion, wanting and not wanting, confines you to live in a world of likes and dislikes.

Greed and hate are not all or nothing states. Jealousy and envy are defilements originating from the three roots. They can range from minor discomfort to all-consuming pathological passion. If I am consumed by jealousy, it means I want to possess a particular person or object and I do not want other people to possess them. I am suspended between wanting and not wanting. This is unwholesome karma, which will lead to unwanted consequences. When I succumbed to greed and aversion, I am living in the house of delusion. When I overcome these unwholesome roots,
I open a pathway to acceptance, surrender, and love.

Right view is the way we see things. This means to be open-minded, to have a clear view of things, not masked by what you want to see. It is not influenced by your false beliefs of what you feel you should see. In the concentric mind model, your beliefs are under your thoughts, which affect your emotions which all affect your perception. You see the world as you believe you should see it. These beliefs in turn are determined by your desires. If you correct these desires all the layers above are corrected, your beliefs, your thoughts, your emotions, and finally your perception of the world. You see what you want to see, you perceive the world as you believe it to be and that often gets you into trouble.

To believe in right view is not enough, it needs to become a conviction. If you say you believe something but do nothing it is meaningless. A conviction is a belief that results in action.

Remember you select these right views. Please do not wait for absolute scientific proof that they are right. Waiting for perfect logical evidence is not having the right view. You do not have time for this and you need to experience the flood of well-being that comes from the right view. If you don't have the correct mundane right view much of your meditation will be in vain. Without the right view, you will not abide in serenity and joy. We live in a society that fundamentally denies the right view, especially the scientific world.

The right view is to have the mind of the Buddha, which means living with compassion and loving-kindness toward all beings. The Dalai Lama summed it up by saying "my religion is loving-kindness."

## Superior Right View

Rebirth: The Buddha taught that when we die we are reborn and that our karma is carried over into future lives. This goes on for many lives until we obtain enlightenment, which liberates us from the cycle of Samsara which is the cycle of birth, life, and death characterized by dukkha. The enlightened state is characterized by peace, joy, and loving-kindness.

Many people have a problem with multiple rebirths because it is not something that is easily tested, like many other of the Buddha's teachings. The Buddha realized he needed to teach this because disciples needed a model of the truths, to live with conviction about the law of karma. If you are skeptical about this representation of the truth, I will address that concern in the appendix of the book.

One's motives for performing noble actions might be the accumulation of meritorious karma, leading to prosperity and success here and now, or a fortunate rebirth, or the enjoyment of celestial bliss in heavenly worlds. Final deliverance from this karmic cycle, however, requires more than a wholesome mundane right view.

The **superior right view**, leading to liberation is the understanding of the Four Noble Truths. The superior right view happens in two stages. It starts with a conceptual understanding of the four noble truths, which are life is suffering, the cause of suffering is desire, remove desire and you remove suffering. The path to this is the Eightfold Noble Path.

The first noble truth is suffering (dukkha), the inherent unsatisfactoriness of all existence intrinsic to all forms of life. Birth is suffering; aging is suffering; sickness is suffering; death is suffering; sorrow, lamentation, pain grief and despair are suffering; associating with unpleasant things is suffering; separation from pleasant things is suffering; not to get what one wants is suffering. In brief, he said the five aggregates of clinging are suffering.

The **five aggregates of clinging** help us understand the nature of our being. The words the Buddha used for the five aggregates are: material form (the body), feelings (emotions), perceptions, mental formulations (thoughts), and consciousness all held together by clinging.

Look again at our earlier concentric model of the human mind for similarities. The Buddha said these five aggregates are dukkha, which brings our whole existence into the range of dukkha. The reason he says that these aggregates are dukkha is that they are impermanent. They change from moment to moment, they arise and fall away again. There is nothing there to cling to as a basis for security. When we desire to cling to them for permanence, they plunge us into suffering.

**The second noble truth**: the Buddha singles out craving as the dominant and most pervasive cause of the origin of suffering. Craving is intimately tied up with ignorance.

Craving produces repeated existence, is bound up with delight and lust, and seeks pleasure here and there, namely, craving for sense pleasures, craving for existence and craving for nonexistence.

The **third noble truth** is that removal of craving is the "solution." This means complete abandonment of all craving is the solution to the end of suffering.

The state of perfect peace that comes when the craving is eliminated is Nirvana (means extinguishing). Nirvana is a state when greed, aversion, and delusion is extinguished.

Super right view is developed in two stages

The first is the conceptual knowledge of the four noble truths. To acquire the right view which accords with the truths requires a clear understanding of their meanings and significance in our lives. When we achieve this the truths have not yet been penetrated, understanding is still defective.

Penetrating the four noble truths: to penetrate the truth and arrive at an experiential realization of the truths, it is necessary to practice meditation. In meditation, you need to strengthen concentration to gain insight into the five aggregates to know their real characteristics of impermanence. When the mind's eye penetrates them clearly, it can shift focus to the unconditioned state of "no-mind". At the same time, these five aggregates are clearly seen, craving stops, and Nirvana is reached.

At this point, one knows for themselves that the Eightfold Noble Path is the way.

Few people have attained this liberation. Thus we can see that the right view is both at the start and the end of the Eightfold Noble Path. We start with the right view conforming to the truths and embark on the threefold journey of moral discipline, concentration, and wisdom. When the training matures, the eye of wisdom opens up penetrating the truths.

## 2. Right Intention

Right intention, is sometimes translated as right thought. Right intention is not merely an intellectual activity but an emotional activity of the mind. It is an attitude of the heart towards the world, and how you experience the world.

It is not immediately obvious why the right intention would follow from the Four Noble truths. If you look closely, the right intention is an obvious extension of the right view. First, you need to understand the right view, which has three important factors in it.

Non-anger or the absence of ill-will

Absence of harmful intentions

Renunciation (non-greed or non-desire)-- real renunciation is not a matter of compelling ourselves to give up things still inwardly cherished, but changing our understanding of them so they no longer bind us.

If you look at the roots of the above, they are non-greed and non-anger which come about by non-delusion. This is a recurring theme of the Buddha's teachings, which helps us have a framework for most of his vast teachings. The Buddha often summarises his teaching by the roots, which are non-greed, non-aversion, and non-delusion.

Before his Enlightenment, the Buddha would examine his thoughts and divide them into unwholesome thoughts of desire, ill-will, and harmfulness, and wholesome thoughts of renunciation (non-desire or surrender to what is), goodwill and harmlessness. He found that unwholesome thoughts led to harm to himself and others, obstructed wisdom, and led away from Nirvana. He found that as he wilfully expelled these thoughts from his mind, it led away from suffering. Whenever wholesome thoughts arose, he understood these to be beneficial, conducive to the growth of wisdom, and an aid to the attainment of Nirvana. Thus he concentrated on strengthening those thoughts that lead to the end of suffering.

In short, out of delusion (misunderstanding) arises greed and aversion. Out of the right view (understanding or wisdom) arises non-greed and non-hatred.

So right intention which arises from the right view is the intention of non-ill will, which is not the same as goodwill. It is the absence of harmful intentions.

We see that themes of greed, aversion, and delusion recur in the Buddha's teachings. So the right view (understanding) is the absence of delusion, which leads to the absence of greed and aversion. Right intention is the presence of non-ill will, non -harmfulness, and non-greed.
We will see that the right intention will lead to right speech and right effort. Right speech is difficult to do intellectually as it happens so fast, but if you develop right intention right speech happens spontaneously. The right effort is also dependent on right intention.
Right intention also fits under the third category of mindfulness where we examine our thoughts to see if they are greedy or not, angry or not, deluded or not. In effect, a right intention is a form of mindfulness practice, and we can see that all components of the Eightfold Noble Path are connected.
As we gain an understanding of the path, we will see that it is designed to purify the mind. It is designed to remove the veil of our egoic thought pattern to reveal who we truly are, which is loving-kindness and compassion. This is the path to awakening from the egoic thought system, defiled by delusions of greed and aversion.

### 3. Right Speech
Speech is used continuously in ordinary life, through the day, and may be more of a challenge to laypeople than

monks. The lay community in particular needs to use speech skilfully.

Right speech is based on right intention. You cannot modulate your speech by preparing it ahead of time, by rehearsing vocabulary, or sentences. You need to respond spontaneously to all kinds of situations.

This is done by sincere effort to cultivate right intention. A heart that has been taught non-ill will, non-cruelty, and renunciation will automatically result in right speech. Your speech is then cleansed from a tendency to hostility and demeaning of others. Because the heart is purified, it does not focus unwisely on the faults of things.

Once you learn renunciation, you will not try to manipulate things falsely with your speech. This can be a challenge even for otherwise good people in sales. It is tempting to fudge the truth to make the sale. It is easy to become manipulative to get something out of people. You probably will be a more successful salesman if you are candid and truthful to your customers. The Buddha wants people to do well in lay life, as far as earning money and having an easy life.

Going back one more step, right intention is based on right view so if you're having trouble with right speech go back and examine right view. To keep track of right speech look at the following.

Abstain from falsehood and speak the truth. There is social pressure to promote yourself or to conceal some aspect of yourself that is faulty.

This does not mean that you blurt out anything that is true. The Buddha says before you speak ask yourself "is it true and is it beneficial?" This does not mean that what you say is always pleasant. It is possible that what you need to say is true and beneficial, but it may be unpleasant for the other person to hear.

There are times when you should not speak the truth, that is to say, you remain silent, but very few times when you should lie. The only times a lie may be karmically permissible, is if it is done with the right view and right intention. One example might be if you are asked the whereabouts of someone when you know the people seeking him want to murder or harm him.

Refrain from harsh speech. Always be pleasant and courteous. What we say, can bring gain or loss, praise or blame, good repute or ill, misery, or happiness. A gentle word can melt the hardest heart, while a harsh word can cause untold agony. Sometimes your speech needs to be firm and uncompromising, and you do need to be skillful. If you have the right view and right intention, this will guide you to right speech.

Refrain from divisive speech. Divisive speech means you try to divide people rather than reconciling them. It could mean slander or tale-telling. Divisive speech, or the desire to sow discord, seems to be common in human society. The karma associated with it is not good, and it will bounce back on you. You will be distrusted, and there will be negative fruits of your divisive speech.

Frivolous speech: People are fond of idle talk, of maliciously disparaging others. The gossip columns promote and laud this practice. Men and women, with time on their hands, indulge in endless chatter, amusing themselves at the expense of others. Frivolous speech is difficult to define but it is pointless speech. The actual word in Pali is sampapalapa, which is an onomatopoeic word that when translated means blah blah blah.

This type of speech is a waste of life, a diffusion of energy, and it is confusing. If you find yourself in the midst of frivolous speech, it is tiring and de-energizing, whereas true speech, or skillful speech, leaves an afterglow and it is energizing.

Lying in our political system is a grave problem. If it becomes pervasive, the entire society can crumble. The Buddha says the karmic penalty for lying is severe. Right speech is just a skill that you need to practice. When you slip up, just pick yourself up and try to do better next time. When right speech deserts you, it is always because your heart was not in the right place. Go back and contemplate right view and right intention to fix this.

If you are sitting in a room full of people, and you truthfully reveal a fault or failing that you have, it allows everybody to relax and drop their defense. The Buddha says the noble person reveals his faults without great encouragement, but it will be difficult to get self-praise out of them. In the lesser person, it will be exactly the opposite. People often think that they should always put their best forward, and constantly promote and advertise themselves, but this is not the way of highly developed people.

## 4. Right Action

Just as right speech is to avoid causing harm with what you say, right action means avoiding causing harm with what you do. So in place of physically hurting others with your actions, you seek to help and protect.

In particular, the Buddha mentions three components of right action.
Abstain from taking the life of any sentient being.
Abstain from taking what is not given.
Abstain from sexual misconduct.

The reason why you abstain from these things is that you have right view. This implies that you understand why you need to abstain from them. Only if you have an understanding of what you are doing, will you be called virtuous.

Fulfilling right action requires both right effort and right mindfulness. You make the effort to both abstain from harming individuals, and you also make the effort to do the opposite, which is to protect them. The minimum requirement is neutrality, which requires mindfulness, and which keeps you lucid, rational, and in an emotionally positive state.
Thus to achieve right action you need right view, right effort, and right mindfulness. Right mindfulness always goes with right effort. Just observing is not right mindfulness, you need to make an effort and do something. So in right action, certain actions, which are recognized as being wrong, must be actively stopped.

The Buddha teaches that we should not kill any sentient being, which in practice implies humans, animals, and insects.

Abstaining from taking what is not given, includes stealing, robbery, snatching, fraudulence, and deceitfulness.

Abstaining from sexual misconduct: the Buddha goes into much detail for both men and women. In general, this would include having sex outside of marriage if you are married, anyone prohibited by convention, like women still under the protection of guardians, relatives, or anyone prohibited by the law of the land, or anyone celibate due to religious vows.

There are extensive sutras written in Buddhism on each of these topics which you can easily find.

If the right view and right intention are well developed, you would generally know intuitively what is right and wrong.


## 5. Right Livelihood

Right livelihood is concerned with ensuring that you earn a living in a righteous way. One should acquire wealth legally, peacefully, without coercion or violence, without trickery or deceit.

The Buddha mentions specific kinds of livelihood, which may bring harm to others and should be avoided: dealing in weapons, dealing in living beings like slavery, prostitution, or even raising animals for slaughter. The wrong livelihood includes practicing deceit, lying, trickery, soothsaying, and usury. Anything that requires a violation of right speech and right action should be off-limits.

On a more subtle level, you may find yourself in a job that requires constant conflict with others. Your job may be so busy that you do not have time for spiritual pursuits like meditation, studying, or retreats. You may have no choice at a certain time in your life, but you should try and correct this.

In summary, any job that requires you to break any of the Eightfold Noble pathway rules, should be avoided.

## 6. Right Effort

Right effort is a critical teaching. A lot of attention is given in the West to mindfulness, but the right effort is ill-understood in many instances. It is tied together with right concentration and right mindfulness. These three are inseparable, and they are the launching pad of the mental culture that leads to insight-wisdom, which in turn is the primary tool for awakening. Without these three, progress is difficult or even impossible. Let us discuss right effort under four headings

1. Prevent unwholesome mental states arising.
2. Eliminate unwholesome mental states that have arisen.
3. Develop wholesome mental states.
4. Deepen and strengthen wholesome mental states.

The first two are negative mental states or emotions that need to be eliminated, and the second two are positive mental states that need to be fostered. So think about building a lovely garden. First, you need to prevent weeds and unwanted plants from growing, and second, you need to remove the weeds that are already there. You also need to plant the desired flowers and fruits and maintain them. Then you need to deepen and strengthen the quality and quantity of the desired plants. You cannot just remain observers of the garden, but you need to make an effort to cultivate a beautiful garden.

1. Prevention of unwholesome mental states: prevention is better than cure and we need to be constantly vigilant to prevent these mental states from arising. Keep a constant eye on things that provoke desire in us, and things that provoke dislike or aversion. We can use the Buddha's technique of looking at the five hindrances which we will discuss in detail in the second heading.

2. Eliminate unwholesome mental states that have arisen: the Buddha suggests that in order to do this, we take a look at the five hindrances. It is not so much about what arrives at the eye and the ear, it is about the consciousness you direct towards that event or happening. It is about the focus and attention you give them. If you focus on things you judge as bad, it produces ill will. If you focus too much on the things you judge as beautiful, that produces craving and desire.

The Buddha related the parable of the criminal who the people were considering releasing.

The king said that he should be tested, by making him walk through the village fairground with a bowl of oil. At the fairground, the most beautiful girl in the village was dancing. There were also unpleasant drunken louts jeering him as he walked. If he made it across the fairground, he was free to go, but if he spilled the oil he would be killed. The same goes with us if we pay too much attention to the ugly things in life, or too much attention to the pleasurable things in life, we will lose our lives of peace and joy.

Society encourages us to focus on these things, constantly look at them critically, be constantly aware of the latest news and developments of these things. This is not what the Buddha tells us to do. This is bad advice if you seek peace.

A technique to do this, said the Buddha, is to consider the five hindrances and find antidotes for them.

**The Five Hindrances**
Sensual desire
Anger or ill will
Sloth and torpor
Worry and restlessness
Doubt

The job of the contemplator or the meditator is to remove these things. How do you do this? The Buddha has some skillful techniques to do this.

Method 1:
Replace with the opposite: the meditator must look at the problem and replace it with the opposite. If you experiencing anger, meditate on it, and make an active effort to replace it with the opposite, which is goodwill. Fill

your thoughts with goodwill. Look for them and promote them and the anger will be displaced. The opposite of desire is the absence of desire, and one way to achieve this is to break down the object into its basic elements of substance, Earth, Water, Air, and Fire. A car is made of metal, glass, and rubber. Remove the glamour from what you desire. Agitation is counteracted using serenity practices. Sloth is counteracted by energy, find some light, splash cold water on your face, do exercise et cetera. Even a death meditation increases energy. For doubt, meditate on serenity through breath meditation. Ask questions of others and introduce clarity to the doubt.

Method 2
Fear and shame: also done by contemplation and meditation. Direct your attention to what should be feared, which are the consequences of indulging in the five hindrances. Fear moving towards dukkha and away from awakening.

Contemplate shame: a young beautiful person looks in the mirror, ready to go out into society and discovers a dead snake around their neck. Certainly, you would remove that snake before you interact with people. Just like this, you should remove the ugly things about your persona as soon as you can. These ugly things of the five hindrances, mar the beauty of your mind, they mar your character. If you are always aggressive, angry, and irritable with people you would work on removing this.
Method 3:
Distraction: if you are having an unwholesome desire for something, distract yourself. The Buddha gives the example of the little bag that all monks carry with their few

little possessions. Unpack it and re-arrange it, he says, to distract yourself. This could also be house-work, watering the garden and the like.

Method 4
The gradual method: he gives the example of the man who is running. He asks himself why am I running? Then he walks. He asks himself why am I walking? Then he sits. He asks himself why am I sitting? Then he lies down. He does not go straight from running to lying down.
The other thing you can do is ask yourself how did it start and what was the trigger? Contemplate and analyze this, it will serve as the distraction and slowly reduce the intensity, until the problem gradually dissolves.

Method 5
Suppression: if all the above fails, you can just grit your teeth and suppress the problem. This is the fifth and the last remedy, and the last resort, but it is better than allowing the hindrance to thrive until you can stop feeding the misinformation factory that is flooding in.

Another general technique that covers all of the hindrances, is to reflect on the impermanence of all these things and this will lessen the importance to you.

If you do this regularly, you will gradually change your personality for the better. The bottom line is to experiment, try different things, but do whatever it takes to overcome the five hindrances sometimes called the five psychic irritations.

**3.** Develop wholesome mental states: these are the instructions for the direction of effort and energy. This is not mere observation, it requires effort to cultivate and maintain the seven factors of awakening. The seven factors are both the path to awakening and the characteristics of an awakened being.

**The Seven Factors of Enlightenment**
Mindfulness
Investigate Dharma
Energy
Joy
Tranquility
Concentration
Equanimity

**Mindfulness:** can be cultivated by paying attention in a specific way, that is in the present moment, and as non-reactively, non-judgementally, and open-heartedly as possible. Mindfulness is the gatekeeper of the mind, it will not just allow anything in there. It filters the contents of your mind for the good. The instruction to mindfulness is to exclude anything that distorts reality, that is all the five hindrances. Mindfulness welcomes two factors in particular serenity and clarity of insight, which accurately reports reality.

**Investigation of the Dharma**: which means the investigation of the reality of existence. We live life with shock and dismay, but if we understood reality, we would not be shocked or dismayed. We contemplate and investigate three characteristics of existence which are anicca= impermanence of all things, dukkha= unsatisfactoriness of all things, anatta= selfless insubstantial nature of existence. We will talk about these later in the book.

**Energy:** this is often naturally produced when you live with mindfulness and investigation. It is interesting and absorbing, which results in you feeling energetic and motivated.

**Joy:** will arise naturally when you are involved in mindfulness, investigation of existence, and energy. It is not reality that supplies joy to you, rather you put joy into reality. En-joy-ment; when you break this word down it means you put joy in, not take it out. Joy comes out of you from inside, it does not come from events outside of you into you. Everything about existence becomes interesting and enjoyable. You become saturated with the joy of curiosity, enquiry, and clarity.

**Tranquility:** once this joy pervades you for a while, you feel serenity, a sense of well-being, and everything is just as it should be, and it is good. It is a beautiful state of serenity, this leads to concentration.

**Concentration:** the mind becomes concentrated, and you experience deepening of serenity into a state of stillness, deep concentration. There is an extraordinary effusion of well-being, both in physical and mental aspects.

**Equanimity**: if all these aspects come together, you experience equanimity, which is a beautiful and perfect balance. You become a kind of witness to things but in complete stillness and wisdom. There is wisdom based equanimity and a concentration based equanimity that fuse into one.

The awakened person can function perfectly well in normal life activities but needs periods of solitude and stillness to maintain, practice, and meditate in this state.

Maintenance and deepening of wholesome mental states

4. Deepening, and bringing to perfection the seven factors of awakening is the most beautiful part of the gardening process. It is akin to watering and attending our beautiful garden. This is where the ultimate fruit of enlightenment is brought to fruition.

Maintaining the seven factors of awakening is a constant practice of the elements of the right effort, using right mindfulness and right concentration until you become a different person. You have transcended the human egoic thought system, and for Christians, this is what is meant by being born again. You die before you die, in other words, your unwholesome being dies and your wholesome being is born.

## 7. Right Mindfulness

Mindfulness is taught everywhere in the West today by many people with different ideas, and usually, they just scratch the surface, but **right** mindfulness is what the Buddha taught. The Pali word Samma is loosely translated as right or correct. It also means "at the service of". So what is right mindfulness at the service of? It is at the service of emotional liberation and the end of suffering. The Buddha teaches that the roots of suffering are desire, hatred, and misunderstanding (greed, aversion, and delusion). So right mindfulness is a technique to overcome these unwholesome roots.

Many secular mindfulness teachers emphasize inner observation of the chaos inside of us, quieting the mind and observing in stillness. Mindfulness is merely an observer for them. That is scratching the surface, and although it is an introduction and good to practice, it is just the beginning, or the first step in the right mindfulness that the Buddha taught, which is in the service of enlightenment.

Right mindfulness is a hired gun, sentry, or guard of the mind. It guards against greed, aversion, and delusion, which are the three poisons that lead to dukkha. It is the gardener who prevents the growth of weeds and unwanted plants, and if they arise removes the weeds. This sentry needs to eliminate judgment, pull the focus into the present moment, view the world with unconditional loving-kindness, and develop and deepen equanimity.

The seminal sutta on mindfulness is "The Four Foundations of Mindfulness" which takes only 10 to 15 minutes to read, and is in the words of the Buddha himself. I recommend that you read it.

The **Four Foundations** or categories of mindfulness that the Buddha said we should examine are

1. The Body (Kaya)
2. Feelings or emotions (Vedana)
3. Mind  states(Citta)
4. Dharma categories—the basic foundations of the teachings of the Buddha.

At the end of each one of these categories, the Buddha inserts a recurring phrase "Just to the extent necessary for the overcoming of covertness and grief for the world." Covertness is greed and grief is aversion.

To do this effectively you need to be able to observe what is happening and understand it, by putting it into one of the four categories, and then examining it for greed, aversion, and delusion, by looking at the five hindrances. To repeat the five hindrances are sensual desire, anger or ill will, sloth or torpor, worry or restlessness, and doubt.

Right mindfulness, needs right effort to be an effective protector of the garden of your mind. The Buddha said that you must practice this with diligence, which means constant vigilance combined with effort.

The observational aspect of mindfulness can be experienced quite easily, but cannot adequately be described in words. It can be pointed to, and what it does can be described, but to know truly what it is, it needs to be experienced.

Definition: mindfulness can be cultivated by paying attention in a specific way, that is in the present moment, and as non-reactively, non-judgmentally, and open-heartedly as possible.

Notice that this definition tells us some of the characteristics of mindfulness but it does not pin it down, because words cannot do that.

Then there is another function to right mindfulness, and that is to plant, and then maintain and deepen and strengthen the beautiful plants in the garden. This is done using right effort to plant maintain and strengthen the 7 factors of enlightenment.

Right effort, right mindfulness, and right concentration all feed off each other, and the more you develop one of them, the more the other two are deepened. The Buddha gives the analogy of three young boys trying to reach some fruit high up in a tree. The only way they can do it, is if the tall boy stands on the strong boy's back and a third boy lends a shoulder for stability, so do right effort, right mindfulness, and right concentration work together to attain the prize. The prize is the wisdom that leads to awakening and the end of suffering.

Mindfulness meditation is a common technique used in Buddhism to achieve an uncluttered mind and to put you into a state open to receiving insight. Mindfulness and Buddhist meditation go hand in hand. See Chapter 5 for Buddhist Meditation

### 8. Right Concentration
Samma Samadhi translated as right concentration is a total absorption trance-like state. It is the state of being totally aware of the present moment; a one-pointedness of

mind. It is the centering of consciousness on a single object. It is the highest state of mental concentration, that a person can achieve while still bound to the body, which unites him with the highest reality. Samma can also be translated as "in the service of" so Samma Samadhi means concentration in the service of the end of suffering.

It differs from meditation in that while concentration is an act to achieve a focused mind, meditation seeks an uncluttered mind. Concentration can focus on your inner world and outer world, while meditation focuses on the inner world only. Meditation can lead to insight and realization and can unclutter the mind in the service of concentration.

Concentration is often achieved by top sportsmen, when they are in the zone, totally concentrating on winning a Wimbledon tennis final for example, or anyone totally concentrated on an activity, like music or other things. This, however, is not **right** concentration. The Buddha called it Micha samadhi, which is samadhi but not in the service of the correct topics. Right concentration means that this "in the zone concentration", is in the service of the end of suffering and enlightenment.

In Buddhism, it is the final factor in the Eightfold Noble Path, that completes the turning of the wheel, back to the wisdom factors, right view, and right intention. It leads to the highest insights, which leads to a complete understanding of the Four Noble truths, the role of desire, aversion, and delusion in dukkha. It brings right view and right intention into fullness, attaining the wisdom which is needed for enlightenment.

Right concentration is an exalted state of mind and of heart, which is only achievable if you develop the first seven factors in the right way.

The Buddha describes four states of intense concentration called Jhanas.

Jhana is translated as training of the mind or meditation. These can only be experienced if you have suppressed the five hindrances. The other seven factors of the Eightfold Noble Path lay the groundwork for right concentration. Jhanic meditation requires that the 5 hindrances are overcome and you need the insight of the other seven factors to be able to do this. In this way, access concentration is developed to move into the first Jhanic state which develops spontaneously. Once a one-pointed concentration is reached, we focus our consciousness onto something pleasant and maintain focus on it. See Chapter 5 on Buddhist Meditation. In brief, the four Jhanas are as follows. They are called Rupa (form) Jhanas and focus on a subject.

1. **First Jhana**: if you maintain the right concentration it will eventually erupt into piti (physical sensation of glee or well-being) and sukha (the emotional component of joy or rapture). A glimpse of this is not good enough and must be sustained. It starts with a calming breath meditation into stillness. You need to recall sensations of joy and pleasure that external things have momentarily given you and then autosuggest them to happen without an external cause. Jhana meditation is a huge relief from the world. It is like the emotion you might feel about overcoming an illness or being freed from crushing debt. It relieves you

from the psychic illness of desire, ill will, torpor, restlessness, and doubt. It is a very pleasant state which once achieved will draw you back again and again.

2. **Second Jhana:** you then focus on the pleasure (e.g.) and bring calm to it, while sustaining that joy. This will bring you to the second Jhana. The background thinking still present in the first Jhana subsides, and you reach a state of tranquility. The physical experience subsides, and your mind focuses on the emotional experience of joy

3. **Third Jhana:** you extend this further to the third Jhana, where the physical component is completely gone and the joy starts to subside toward contentedness and tranquility.

4. **Fourth Jhana:** the contentedness subsides and you enter into a state of quiet stillness. There is no pleasure and no pain, and we call this state equanimity. It is a neutral state of complete balance. The Buddha called it uphekka (equanimity). This is likened to a breathless stillness and in fact, scientists measuring the breathing rate of monks in this state show that they breathe at 3 breaths per minute (normal respiratory rate is 12 to 15 breaths per minute).

Now you are in a state where you have removed the ego and are completely open to insight and wisdom. In this state, you can do any insight practice better (like vipassana). So the four Jhanas are a warm-up for insight practices on any aspect of reality or the dharma. For example, you may do insight practice on the three universal truths of anicca (impermanence), dukkha, and anatta (no-self) which is key to awakening. It is here that experiential wisdom can be honed, and right view and right intention perfected, which is the direct path to awakening.

There are four even higher concentrations states often call the higher four Jhanas or Arupa Jhanas, which are formless meditations, and which yield even more insight and wisdom. Briefly, they consist of the following.

1. The sphere of infinite space.
2. The experience of limitless consciousness
3. The experience of nothingness
4. The experience of neither perception nor non-perception.

Each of these states is subtle, meaning there is no
body-awareness and these are just the refinements of the fourth Rupa Jhana.

There are, of course, many paths to the top of the mountain. Some people say build up the concentration first and then move on to insight. Others say go straight for insight practices and build up the concentration as you go. It also seems that Jhanas 1 to 4 are sufficient, and 5 to 8 is an optional extra.

The purpose of the Jhanas are to make insight (wisdom) practices possible, and the dharma wheel turns to ripen the wisdom factors of right view and right intention. The Jhanas are not an end in themselves, as some people teach. It is this insight wisdom, which leads to the end of suffering and awakening. The eight spokes of the dharma wheel, are all needed, to provide stability so that it can turn.

This was a way described by the Buddha to purify your mind and obtain a clear happy state, unencumbered by the 5 hindrances. There are certainly people who have got to this state without using this exact practice of Jahnas, so bear in mind, it was how the Buddha guides us to do it to help us. The purpose of getting to this state of right concentration is to be able to see reality and develop wisdom about the Universal truths and other dharma teachings, which leads to the end of suffering and awakening.

The Buddha left a lot of instructions about how to investigate reality and obtain insight wisdom. See chapter 5 on Insight Wisdom Practices.

# Chapter 3

# The Three Universal Truths

Also known as the three characteristics of all phenomena. These are vital truths that need to be understood and penetrated on the pathway to the end of suffering.

**Anicca (impermanence: not stable)**
**Anatta (no-self; empty of inherent existence)**
**Dukkha (unsatisfactoriness or suffering).**

Anicca: can be translated as impermanence of all things, but another translation that makes sense is "the inability to maintain anything to one's satisfaction". These are just two facets of the same truth, that cannot adequately be put into words, and as usual, words are just pointers to this truth that needs to be penetrated.

Even though we cannot maintain anything in our lives to our satisfaction, many of us believe we can, and continually try to do this anyway. We crave to make something a permanent reality, and each time we fall short of this, we suffer dukkha. Unless you realize impermanence on all levels, consciously, subconsciously, and deeply you will have dukkha. Until you completely accept or surrender to reality, you will not end suffering. When you fully appreciate this truth, you will see that craving is futile.

Anatta: Pali-anatta or Sanskrit anatman: means no-self.

This at first can seem problematic to understand, but once you see it for yourself it is a simple teaching.

An analogy that might help: you are told by someone that your home is radioactive. You trust that person and you believe it implicitly at first. You then get hold of a tool to verify radio-activity; -a Geiger counter. You take the Geiger counter and search for the radioactivity in every room, and every nook and cranny in your house, but you don't find anything and you discover that what you believed was there, is false. You discover "no radioactivity".

Likewise, we have all developed a false belief of the self. We think we know who we are. When we say the word "I" we think we have an idea who "I" is, but the Buddha gives us a Geiger counter to look for this "I". This Geiger counter is the dharma, which culminates in insight-wisdom. This wisdom shows you that there is indeed "no-self" that is real or permanent.

The Buddha introduced Anatta suggesting there is no enduring self. Then Nagarjuna came along and said, not only is there no enduring self, there is no enduring thing, which he denoted as Sunyata (emptiness). I think no enduring self (Anatta) encompasses no enduring thing (Sunyata) as all things are a reflection of the self.

The first meaning of emptiness is called "emptiness of essence," which means that phenomena [what we experience] have no inherent nature by themselves." The second is called "emptiness in the context of Buddha Nature," which sees emptiness as endowed with qualities of the awakened mind, like wisdom, bliss, compassion, and so on.

The three universal truths or three characteristics of all phenomena are all intimately connected, and the more deeply you understand one, the more you will penetrate the other two. The Buddha teaches us that to penetrate the truth, we first need to purify our minds. Much later in Buddhism, this process was labeled "the first turning of the wheel".

This happens by studying the four noble truths and the eightfold noble path. It is only the wholesome, happy, tranquil, mind that can understand and penetrate the three universal truths correctly. It is only the mind that has a firm understanding of and has practiced right view, right intention, right speech, right action, right livelihood, right effort, right mindfulness, and right concentration, that can understand the teachings of the dharma and the truth of the teaching of the three universal truths.

If our relationship with others is fractious and judgmental, it means we are clinging to our "self", or our egoic thought pattern. Our attachment to our false self or ego is strong and difficult to break. In this state right understanding is not possible. As we chip away and remove the five hindrances of sensual desire, ill will, sloth, restlessness, and doubt, which have their roots in greed, aversion, and ignorance, we begin to uncover who we really are.

We find that who we really are, is compassion and loving-kindness. Once we have turned the wheel and we have a happy, clear, and bright mind we are ready to turn it again to penetrate the universal truths and gain wisdom. The more wisdom we gain the more compassionate we become. The more compassionate we become, the more wisdom we gain. Buddhism is like a turning wheel, that as we move forward, we see that all of the aspects of the Dharma work together to propel the wheel.

Anatta: (no-self) is not a thing that we attain, rather it is just the removal of a wrong view, brought about by ignorance of reality. It is using our Geiger counter to show what we thought was there, is not really there. We see that what we thought was our self, is just a concept, in fact, it is an illusion. Once we gain this wisdom of right view and right intention, it is strengthened.

If we look at our life and our experiences in the world carefully, and the global word we used to describe ourselves "I" or "me", cannot be pinned down, as every aspect of it changes or is changeable.

Let us look carefully under five headings called 5 Khandas or aggregates.

**Physical**: our body is very different when we were a child, than it is now and will be in the future, and one day it will dissolve into the elements, which are the building blocks of the universe, building blocks of physical creation.
If someone has all their teeth removed, or lose one of their limbs, or have plastic surgery, they will look very different, but there's something within, that remains unchanging. Mindful meditation on the body is a tool we can use to see this truth. We could also use meditation on the death of the body to realize this truth.
**Emotions:** these are fickle and changing and range from all the derivatives of fear like anxiety, worry, anger,

and numerous other negative emotions and all the derivatives of love, like compassion, generosity, and a myriad of other emotions.

**Perception:** our five senses perceive things based on our beliefs about the object. If our belief about the object changes our perception changes. For example, a small child given a pen might believe it is a chew toy, or a drumstick, or even a spear, and as we get older we come to know it as a writing instrument. Our perception is determined by our beliefs.

**Thought:** the thoughts that arise, also stem from our deep-seated beliefs, and these are also fickle and changing.

**Consciousness:** which is our awareness again depends on our beliefs, which affect our thoughts and emotions so even that changes.

We believe that accumulating life experiences, which we perceive as good, and lessening ones we perceive as bad, will enhance the sense of self. The point is that nothing that we used to define the word "I" is constant, permanent, or unchanging.

If we take our "Geiger counter" to find these things, we find that they are not real. They are all illusions. This self that we believe is who we are, does not exist. The Buddha calls this truth anatta or no-self. This is a negative teaching about what we are not. In later sutta's the Buddha talks about our luminous self which is compassion and loving-kindness. This is what we are, but it takes awakening to penetrate this truth and know who we are.

The Advaita's atman and the Christian soul and the Buddha's "no-self", are all pointers to the same truth.

When the Buddha talks about objects of phenomena being empty, he means that we are perceiving these objects with our "false self" and because the false self does not exist, the objects are empty, that is to say, they do not exist without our false self's perception. They are not inherently part of what is real.

When the Buddha said that the nature of all phenomena is emptiness we lose the true meaning in translation into English. He did not mean that they are truly empty like a vacuum, he meant beyond our ability to perceive with our senses or to conceptualize. A better word might be inconceivable or unknowable, and it also implies a sense that anything can happen or anything can arise. Emptiness is the space with unlimited potential. Quantum physics has shown us the tiniest particles cannot be pinned down, and that they have many potentialities.

Out of this indefinable unknowable basis all thoughts, emotions, and sensations perpetually arise. Because the nature of our mind is emptiness, we possess the capacity to experience a potentially unlimited variety of thoughts, emotions, and sensations.

## The Three Turnings of the Wheel

This was not a term used by the Buddha himself, but rather refers to a framework for understanding the sutta stream of the teachings of Buddhism, originally devised by the Yogachara school in 400 AD. It later became prevalent in a modified form in Tibetan Buddhism and related traditions. In essence, the first turning of the wheel is accepted as the first discourse at Deer Park where the

Buddha taught the Four Noble Truths and the Eightfold Noble Path.

**First turning**: In the first turning of the wheel, we need some wisdom to set out in the correct direction by having an idea of what right view and right intention are. We then purify our minds by practicing right morality and ethics, by practicing right speech, action, and livelihood. In other words, we purify our thoughts, words, and deeds. This leads us to the right concentration and focus, by making right effort, mindfulness, and concentration including meditation.

**Second turning:** This right concentration, in turn, fortifies our wisdom strengthening right view and right intention and as the Buddha says, allows us to penetrate these things. Now armed with our new improved wisdom we can perform the morality factors better and we can direct concentration better and finally gain the wisdom that leads us to awaken which we call the third turning of the wheel.

One of the key texts of the second turning is The Heart Sutta. The motivation for gaining wisdom is to benefit all sentient beings, so we could say, that the motivation for wisdom is compassion. It turns out that as wisdom deepens, so does compassion and vice versa.

The other aspect of wisdom that develops is the appreciation that form is emptiness. What that means, is the objects around us do not inherently exist on their own. They are empty of accidents because they only exist because of cause and conditions. They exist only because we perceive them. So form is empty, but the Buddha also said emptiness is form. What does that mean?

What that means is that emptiness is not a separate thing. Say I have an object in my hand and a toss it way, I am not left with emptiness, because emptiness is a property of the object.

**Third turning:** This purifies the mind enough to largely overcome the 5 hindrances and practice the 7 factors of enlightenment, and brings the mind to peace and equanimity from where insight practices can help penetrate anatta, anicca, and dukkha and deepen the understanding enough to strengthen wisdom which in turn strengthens and purifies right view and right intention.

The third turning is often called "mind-only", which means the mind is the only thing you need to work on. When you experience form, the only place is in your mind. If you change your mind view, you change your experience. In effect, you create the world that you live in. In this way, you see the world as the Buddha saw it, and now because you have Buddha nature your experience changes from dukkha to compassion and unconditional loving-kindness.

If we can apply this to an object, and realize the perception of the object is projected onto the object by you, we can apply this to another human being. If you encounter an annoying person that makes you angry, you can employ the same mindfulness technique. Ask yourself, "where does that experience of anger come from?"
I cannot change the behavior of an annoying person. The only thing I can change is my mind, and hence my

personal experience. If I change my mind, I change my experience from dukkha to peace. The second turning gives us an understanding of the object, and the third turning gives us an understanding of the subject, and each of them is consistent with what we learned in the first turning.

The third turning is when our wisdom develops to the point where we realize the absolute truth of the dharma, from where we can enter into the four stages of enlightenment. All these teachings do appear in the original Buddha Sutta's but were not labeled as such until hundreds of years later. The turnings of the wheel of dharma is a useful algorithm to use in the practice of Buddhism and gives a good framework to understand the path, but it was not a specific thing outlined by the Buddha himself.

These three turnings refine your wisdom to the point where you can awaken. You become a new being. You die before you die, meaning your egoic thought system is transcended and as Christians would say, you are born again.

Whether you get there by following the path outlined by the Buddha, by Jesus, or other spiritual paths, you arrive at the same place. You might name it enlightenment, you might name it the Kingdom of Heaven which is within. You might name it God-realization, or self-realization. Words are just pointers, experiential wisdom or a deep knowing is reality.

The Buddha himself taught his disciples to be tolerant of other religions. He said when one lights a candle from the flame of another candle, the first candle does not lose its light. Instead, the two lights glow more brightly together. It is the same with the great religions of the world. The Buddha however outlined his teachings in a methodical step by step manner. The dharma is a detailed manual of the steps you need to take to end suffering. It gives concrete steps you can take, and see for yourself that they are true.


**The Three Jewels**
Sometimes referred to as the three refuges.
1. Take refuge in the Buddha
2. Take refuge in the dharma (teachings of the Buddha)
3. Take refuge in the sangha (Buddhist community monks and nuns)


Take refuge in the Buddha, means we should care about what he taught. There is no harm in honouring the Buddha by doing prostrations, but your focus should be on his teachings and trying to emulate him and achieve a Buddha-nature. In Buddhism, you do not hand responsibility for your awakening to a saint or a deity, you do it yourself by following the Buddha's teachings.

Take refuge in the dharma, means to read, understand, and put into practice the teachings of the Buddha.

Take refuge in the sangha. The Buddha realized, that most of us need mentoring and help from other members of the community to stay on the path. By teaching each other, we learn. By learning with each other, we teach. The teacher and learner are one.

The Buddha, the dharma, and sangha together possess qualities that can lead us to enlightenment and the end of suffering.

# Notes

# Chapter 4

# The Four Sublime States

In Buddhism, these are sometimes called the four immeasurables, or the four divine states, or the four directions.

Metta –unconditional loving-kindness
Karuna—Compassion

Mudita—sympathetic joy
Upekkha—equanimity

These are mental states or qualities, cultivated by Buddhist practice. This is a huge and vital aspect of Buddhist teachings. This is where the rubber meets the road, and it is the aim of Buddhist teachings, which is to end suffering and live permanently in these mental states. These are recurring themes in the suttas of the Buddha. All the rules and lists are pointers to reach these states permanently, and once you do, the rules are no longer needed as you will automatically follow them.

These states will be the result of following the four noble truths and the Eightfold Noble pathway. The Buddha tells us that this is our true nature, and this is who we are. We just have to scrape away the layers of ignorance and wrong view to reveal this truth. On occasions, the Buddha refers to this as our luminous self.

They should not be places that we visit occasionally, or relegate to meditation, rather our mind should become thoroughly saturated with them. They should become our inseparable companions, and we should become mindful of them in all our activities.

In the Metta sutta it says, "when standing, walking, sitting, lying down, wherever he feels free of tiredness, let him establish well this mindfulness. This, it is said, is the divine abode"

To achieve these states, in most cases, we shall have to use these four qualities not only as principles of conduct and objects of reflection but also as subjects of methodical meditation. We saw these put into practice in the four Jhanas of right concentration. These Jhanas are temporary states used for practice, whereas enlightenment means that we live in these states permanently. Detailed methods of doing these kinds of meditation are available in Buddhist instruction on meditation.

In loving-kindness meditation, we say to ourselves, "Just as I wish to be happy and free from suffering, so may that being, may all beings be happy and free from suffering". We start by choosing an easy subject, someone alive and someone we like and someone we are not sexually attracted to. We expand this to disagreeable people, and then to evil people who may be our enemies. We can do the same thing for compassion, sympathetic joy, and equanimity.

## Metta (loving-kindness)

Unconditional love without the desire to possess is the highest love. It is a love embracing all beings, small and great, far and near, be it on Earth, in the water, or in the air. It is love embracing the noble-minded or the low minded, good or evil. Appreciate that there is only love, anything else is just a cry for help. The Buddha named this kind of love, the liberation of the heart, the most sublime beauty, and said the highest manifestation of love is to show the world the path leading to the end of suffering.

Loving-kindness cannot coexist with the five hindrances of sensual desire, ill will, torpor, restlessness, or doubt. It can exist in the presence of pain, but only once the five hindrances have been overcome.

The state of metta is a pleasurable one, it enhances mindfulness, wisdom, energy, and tranquility. It is not a personal thing and does not rely on other people or outside circumstances. It is a fire filled with energy. The Buddha said it is a fire not dependant on external wood or other materials. Those fires are ephemeral and difficult to keep going, but inner fire requires no wood and is far superior. If you rely on things outside of you to give you pleasure, they come and go, they change and are not reliable. If your pleasure comes from inside of you, by cultivating metta, it is reliable and does not come and go.

## Karuna (Compassion)

Insight into the general law of suffering, not an isolated incident of suffering, is the real foundation of compassion. If we truly penetrate this truth we will be compassionate toward all beings who are suffering. Not only that, we will be compassionate to people who are happy now, but act with an evil and deluded mind because we know they are cultivating the seeds of great suffering. Compassion is not being dragged down into experiencing the other person's suffering, it is an empathetic recognition and acknowledgment of their suffering.

Through compassion, the fact of suffering remains present in our mind, even at times when we are personally free from it. It gives us the rich experience of suffering, thus strengthening us to meet it prepared when it does befall us. We will meet that suffering with equanimity, which is serene acceptance of what is. If we have no compassion, it means we do not see the suffering of others, we are wrapped up in our own small grief or joy.

The compassion of a wise man does not render him a victim of that suffering. His thoughts, words, and deeds are full of pity, but it does not waver, he remains serene and calm. If in any other state, how could he help?

Again, the Buddha says that the highest compassion is to show the path to the end of suffering.

### Mudita (Sympathetic joy)

Not only should we be compassionate towards their suffering, but we should also rejoice in the joy of others. Joy will be enriched by sharing in another's happiness as if it were your own. Let us teach people to seek and find real joy within themselves, and to rejoice with the joy of others.

The Buddha's teaching is sometimes wrongly considered to be a doctrine of diffusing melancholy. This is far from true. The Dharma leads, step by step, to even purer and loftier happiness. Noble and sublime joy helps us extinguish suffering. A joyful mind leads to the right concentration and wisdom, not a mind depressed by grief. Sympathetic joy is a type of energy. Sympathetic joy is sublime nobility of heart and intellect, which knows, understands, and is willing to help.

The Buddha says that the highest sympathetic joy is to show the world the path that leads to the end of suffering.

### Upekkha (Equanimity)

Equanimity is perfect, unshakable balance of mind, rooted in insight. It is a serene acceptance of what the Universe presents to us, coloured with a background of loving-kindness. It is a mental state, which is difficult to describe in words, as words can only point to it. Only in tasting it, in achieving it, will you truly know what it is.

There are two faces of equanimity that need to be looked at. The first is the mental state that we achieve in Jhana meditation. We saw in right concentration that equanimity comes about in the fourth Jahna. This is not a state that most normal people can reach, it requires something supernormal, but it is possible with right effort. We read that in the time of the Buddha, that many monks and many lay people achieved the fourth Jahna in meditation. In some Buddhist traditions today, it is made out to be a one in a million occurrence. If you believe this, then that will be true for you.

When reached in meditation, it is a profound breathless stillness. You feel as if you are not breathing at all, and you may wonder if you are still alive in this world. Monks meditating in the fourth Jahna are measured at three or fewer breaths per minute. Part of this is the body's decreased requirement for oxygen in this profound state of stillness. The brain uses 20% of the oxygen at rest, and it is thought that the oxygen requirement in the whole body is decreased. To get to this state requires right effort, right mindfulness, and right concentration. Meditation, in a way, is preparation for living your daily life.

The second face of equanimity is in your everyday life. If we look at life, we notice how it moves between contrasts:

successes and failures, loss and gain, praise, and blame. Our heart responds to happiness and sorrow, delight and despair, satisfaction and disappointment, cast about uncontrollably, as if in a rough sea. For us, this world gives us scanty joy, amid sickness, suffering, and death.

Equanimity frees us from this, and it comes about by hard, deliberate training. Wisdom is a pre-requisite. We have to penetrate the understanding of dukkha and karma. We have to understand that we reap what we sow. We have to clearly understand that present suffering comes out of past thoughts, words, or deeds. If we understand this, we can bear the suffering with serene tranquility and know that the way out of this is to overcome the five hindrances and nurture the seven factors of enlightenment. We cannot change our past behavior, but we can change our present thoughts, words, and deeds knowing that it will lead to good karma. The answer to suffering is to do good deeds, which plants the seeds for the end of suffering. With this knowledge and the penetration of anicca, anatta, and dukkha we can accept the vicissitudes of life with serene tranquility, which is equanimity.

This also applies to things like fame and wealth. These imposters can also lead to much suffering if we do not treat them with equanimity. We may lose them or even just fear to lose them and then desire aversion, and ignorance creeps in, and dukkha results.

Equanimity is not neutral apathy, it is based on vigilant presence of mind, not on indifferent dullness. It is an active emotion. It is coloured with a background of loving-kindness. It is a subtle, skillful state of mind, which has to be developed by hard and deliberate training. Once realized, you do not need to keep producing it by exertion again and again. If this were the case, it would be defeated by the hardships of life. Rather, it is like riding a bicycle over a steep hill. It requires effort to get to the top, but once over the hill it just requires steering the bicycle with little effort and the pedals turn easily.

For the Arahant(fully enlightened being) to establish equanimity as an unshakeable state, one has to give up all possessive thoughts of "mine", beginning with little things and then progressing to possessions and then things that one's whole heart clings to. One also has to give up all egoistic thoughts of "self", beginning with a small section of one's personality, with qualities of minor importance, but progressing to emotions and aversions that one regards as the centre of one's being, fully detaching from these things. To the degree that we forsake thoughts of "mine" and "self", equanimity will enter our hearts. The Buddha's teaching on "no-self" will guide us to perfect equanimity. Although equanimity is the crown of the sublime states, it cannot operate alone but to be perfected it needs the other three.

Old Zen Parable to illustrate Equanimity
*There was this poor old farmer. He had a single horse and a teenage son, and one day his horse ran away. A bunch of neighbors came over to the farmer and said, "Oh, how awful. I'm sorry you lost your horse."*

*And the old man said, "Maybe. Who know? It could be good or bad." The neighbors just left. They didn't know what to make of his response.*

*A few days later the horse came back and two wild horses came with it. And the neighbors came by and they were rejoicing.*

*"That's so great! Now you have three horses!"*

*The farmer said, "Maybe. Who knows? It could be good or bad."*

*The neighbors left again, probably judging him at this point. A few days later, the man's son was riding one of the horses and he fell off and broke his leg. The neighbors came over again, offering condolences to the old man. His son wouldn't be able to work in the fields anymore.*

*And the old farmer again said, "Maybe. Who knows? It could be good or bad."*

*A few days later the army came to town. Every young man in the village was being forced to go to war. It would be incredibly dangerous and they would be unlikely to ever come home.*

*But they couldn't take the farmer's son. He had a broken leg, so he got to stay behind.*

## The Inter-relations of the Four Sublime States

These four sublime states work together skilfully to subtly regulate and refine each other into perfection.

Unconditional love prevents compassion from turning into partiality or aversion against the excluded side of the story.

Love prevents equanimity from becoming a dull disinterest and imparts warmth and fervor to it, strengthening equanimity's power of keen penetration and wise restraint.

Compassion prevents love and sympathetic joy from forgetting the greater suffering in the world, and until all humanity becomes enlightened dukkha will return. Compassion prevents love and sympathetic joy from turning into self-satisfied complacency. Compassion stirs them to widen their field and look for fresh nourishment and helps them grow into boundless states.

Sympathetic joy holds compassion back from being overwhelmed by the suffering of the world. Sympathetic joy soothes the painful burning in the compassionate heart and keeps it away from melancholic brooding. It prevents sentimentality that weakens and de-energizes the mind and the heart. Sympathetic joy develops compassion into active energetic sympathy.

Sympathetic joy gives to equanimity the mild serenity that softens its stern appearance. It allows one to smile, despite its deep knowledge of the world's suffering.

Equanimity rooted in insight is the guiding and restraining power of the other 3 insights. It gives them direction and sees that the directions are followed in service of the final goal of awakening. Equanimity, which means even-mindedness, gives to love an even unchanging firmness and loyalty. It endows love with patience. Equanimity endows compassion with unwavering courage and fearlessness in the face of misery and despair. To the active side of compassion, equanimity imparts calm, firm wisdom, indispensable to those who practice the difficult art of helping others. It adds patient devotion to the work of compassion.

So we see the four sublime states of metta, karuna, mudita and upekkha are all interlinked and need to be skillfully blended together on the path to awakening.


**The Five Inner Faculties (strengths)**
1. Faith (Saddha)
2. Energy (Viriya)
3. Mindfulness (Sati)
4. Concentration (Samadhi)
5. Wisdom (Panna)
Equanimity prevents stagnation so that watchful mindfulness(3) harmonizes the warmth of faith(1) with the penetrative keenness of wisdom(5). It balances the strength of will (2 energy ), with the calmness of mind(4 Samadhi), and leads us to attain the mind of the Buddha.

# Chapter 5

# Buddhist Meditation

These days many assume that Buddhism and meditation go hand-in-hand. In the past, many Buddhist traditions have focused on cultivating moral behaviour, preserving the Buddha's teachings, and acquiring the good karma that comes from generous giving. They have not doubted that one can live a worthwhile and authentic Buddhist life, without meditating, aiming not towards awakening, but toward a fortunate rebirth. There is a general belief, however, especially among Theravadans, that enlightenment cannot be reached without meditation. Multiple types of meditation have developed over the years. In this book, I am going to try and crystallize meditation as the Buddha himself taught it.

The Buddha described two benefits of meditation
1. Samantha—tranquility of mind or calming of the mind
2. Vipassana—insight meditation
In modern times, many people separate these two benefits into different types of meditation, but in fact, there is no real disconnect between them. We know that the Buddha practiced breath meditation on the night of his enlightenment and throughout his whole life.
Meditation is easier than you think. You can do it anywhere. The essence of it is awareness, that is, knowing what you are thinking, feeling, or doing. It is in essence a non-judgmental awareness. It does not necessarily require emptying the mind of all thoughts, or intense exhausting concentration. Just be aware of something and maintain it in the present moment.

Breath Meditation
The Buddha used breath meditation not only for mental calmness and clarity but also for emotional development and insight.
1. Inhalation: feel the cool air flowing through your nostrils into the nasal cavity. Just notice it and do not try to control it.

Exhalation: notice warmer air on exhalation, feel the texture of it.

Think of the nasal cavity as a receptacle for clean cool air, which cools the mind relieving it of anxiety. Breath meditation is in air element meditation. Just keep bringing your focus back to the breath until you calm your mind. Some people teach this as the focus and endpoint of this type of meditation.

Induction of joy: this is an important aspect of breath meditation. You need to actively induce or persuade joy to pervade your whole body. Suggest to yourself that joy be introduced, and once it is there, induce it to stay and flood your whole body. After that try and refine that joy into tranquility and stillness. Fill all your heart and your mind with joy, and a sense of well-being in the body will follow.

Active inducement is a skill that you develop and cultivate. If you do not know how to do this, and you just rely on chance, it is very unlikely that it will happen. This is the first half of breath meditation and it is as far as many people go. This alone can transform your life. Start with 20 minutes a day and try and work up to 40 minutes a day. It can be an antidote to general anxiety, general worry, self-loathing, and anger. It can become something that you look forward to and cannot live without.

You learn to shut down the endless production of thought. This is mind cultivation, it is a gardening process to remove weeds and promote good emotions.

The Buddha wanted you to do this as preparation to move forward from the seventh factor of mindfulness to enter the eighth factor of the Noble pathway, which is the right concentration, which leads to the four Jhanas. This starts with joy and then you learn to refine it to serenity and finally equanimity.

These are emotional states which you train your body to enter and which do not depend on circumstances around you. He wanted you to gain true Samadhi, for which right concentration is a poor translation. It is profound ease, rapture, and has been called divine consciousness. We are trying to let go of our memory structures, there is no analysis of your life. There is no remembering of your life. You are not doing anything to analyze the future, you are in the present moment. You want to achieve joy, which is not caused by focusing on anything in the past or the future.

If you do not know that this is the goal, it is very unlikely that it will happen by chance. This is a skill that we need to learn, and we need to be able to recreate it each time we meditate. The Buddha was brief on what to achieve, but he specifically talked about the introduction of joy, interest, and energy. In particular, no discursive activity must be present, that is thoughts about the past or future. He said your entire body should be suffused with positive emotion. It starts with the mind, then the heart and body follow.

Sometimes right concentration is described as one-pointed which is another unfortunate translation. It sounds like the laser concentration, but actually, it means oneness with the experience. You may have experienced it as a teenager in love. A star tennis player does not think of his grip and the mechanics of his stroke when he is in the zone, he is one with what he is doing. Likewise, in this meditation, you are immersed in the activity and no part of you is left out of this. When you are not fully present, only part of you is paying attention, you are a divided person, not a whole person.

This can become a skill, a refuge for you that is available to you throughout your life. With it, a new richness, colour, and depth unfold in your life. This is the aim of breath meditation, and it is not complete until you can enter the supernormal state. Breath meditation is not simply a mindfulness meditation. It is a bridge into Samma samadhi, which means concentration in the service of enlightenment.

So breath meditation can be the springboard into the first Jhana. The **five factors** of the first Jhana are

1. **Vitakka---** initial application of attention, some times it is thinking, but in breath meditation is attention on the breath.

2. **Vicara--** sustaining this attention on the breath

3. **Piti--** inducing an emotion of joy, gladness, verging on rapture.

4. **Sukha--** happiness with the body is free from pain and there may be a feeling of warm pleasure in the body.

5. **Ekagghata--** one oneness or complete wholehearted immersion, some times inadequately called one-pointed concentration.

People sometimes say you need to see light, but this is not true. This is an air meditation and the lightness refers to a light airy feeling. This is clearly not a visual meditation. Attaining the mental state of the first Jhana is immensely beneficial. We then will gradually learn to transmute this joy into serenity, and finally, equanimity which is the fourth Jhana. The fourth Jhana is a state of breathless stillness. Some people don't know what joy is, it's been a long time since they experienced it. If you have to ask, it is probably not joy. Ask for more. If it is not happening for you—practice, practice, and "fake it until you make it".

In summary, do not think of breath meditation as purely an observational mindfulness technique, that is just the start, a springboard into "state of mind" or emotional training.

**Vipassana Meditation**
What is the relationship between breath meditation in the samadhi form, and the Vipassana reflective meditation which is a contemplative practice.

These days there are many meditation courses called Vipassana meditation. Generally, this meditation is directed away from deep samadhi, Jhana meditation, or they go past it to Vipassana which just means to see clearly.

The samadhi argument, however, feels that reaching this deep state of joy, in itself, allows one to see clearly. The feeling is, that the deeper mind wants to speak to you, but your mind is talking all the time. You are too noisy and distracted to hear the wisdom from the deeper mind. Samadhi puts your mind into a joyful, tranquil state and allows your mind to penetrate the nature of reality. Samadhi removes the noise and allows the deeper mind to understand the characteristics of all phenomena, which are impermanence, unsatisfactoriness, and no-self. We have heard these truths many times, and they sound wise, but it does not transform us because samadhi is not there.

The Vipassana School say that samadhi and Jhana meditation is too difficult to attain, and that it is extremely rare for people to attain this. They, therefore, skip this step and go straight to reflection on reality and other categories of the dharma.

In the suttas, however, it tells us that many of the Buddha's disciples, both monastic and lay, attained the four Jahnas. Maybe it is possible to skip samadhi, but it is not what the Buddha taught or practiced. He taught the progression of making the right effort, practice mindfulness, which leads to samadhi. He taught that samma samadhi consisted of attaining the four Jahnas, which puts you in a position to penetrate wisdom. In other words, clear insight is the result of doing this kind of meditation.

Just a word on the pandemic of modern life, which is anxiety, worry, and doubt. You are told just to calm down, but no one tells you how. You need to repeatedly practice breath meditation and get good at it. This takes time and effort, and ideally, you practice it when you are not anxious, worried, or in doubt, so that when you are it comes easily.

One way to know if you are in a calm enough state is to measure your respiration rate. Do your meditation and start a clock, count say 34 breaths (in and out), then look at the clock and work out your respiration rate per minute. You should be able to get to four or less per minute. This is an objective measurement tool, to help you develop a proper meditation technique. When you are meditating, stay in this state as long as you can, and as you come out pose the question that you want to be answered.

Whatever problems or doubts remain, should be discussed with a wise spiritual mentor who knows you. Take refuge in the Sangha.

## Loving Kindness Meditation-Metta

In Buddhism, there are many objects we can focus on when we meditate. The simplest meditation is objectless meditation, which is a mindfulness practice where we just observe the comings and goings of the mind, as non-judgmentally as possible, resting in the "isness" of awareness. The perception of the five senses can be used as objects to meditate on, to calm and focus the mind, but I will not go into those here. Loving-kindness meditation, however, is an important object meditation, and it makes sense. When asked about his religion, the Dalai Lama said that his religion is loving-kindness. This is what lies at the core of Buddhism, and it is where the path is leading you.

The dharma first concentrates on removing the roots of suffering, which are aversion, craving, and ignorance, but the goal of this is to lead you into a state of loving-kindness and tranquility. It, therefore, makes sense to try and emulate this mental state in meditation practice. It is a form of emotional training. Also, in a state of joy, our mind is not clouded by a negative thought, and we are more open to insight and wisdom. Joy and wisdom go hand in hand. They feed off each other.

When we practice loving-kindness meditation, we will see the benefits both for ourselves and others. Loving-kindness cannot coexist with the five hindrances, so it is both the training to overcome these and training toward the seven factors of enlightenment. Metta is a mind state that grows all through the Eightfold Path, and should not be thought of as a separate element. Loving-kindness is a constant theme in many suttas. It is at the heart of right view and right intention. It helps develop right speech and right action and right livelihood, and it is what we are trying to achieve in right effort, right mindfulness, and right concentration.

Different techniques for this meditation are widely available. It is good to start with a stillness practice, like breath meditation, and then proceed to induce a feeling of loving-kindness. Start with yourself and then move on to someone alive who you know and respect, perhaps a spiritual mentor. Make sure it is not someone you are sexually attracted to, so someone of the same sex might be good. Expand this to friends and then people who you have neutral feelings for, and then on to disagreeable people and even evil people who you consider your enemy. Gradually expand this feeling of unconditional loving-kindness, to all beings and creatures in all six directions. May they be happy, may they be healthy, may they be safe, may they live with ease, is what you can mentally imagine.

A variant on this is the Tonglen meditation, which is a Tibetan variant on loving-kindness. Tonglen means giving and taking—taking another's pain, and giving them love.

Imagine someone that you want to help. Perhaps it is a friend or a loved one. Focus intently on this person and their struggle.

Breathe in. As you do, focus on the heaviness of their negative energy, and on the things that ail them. Imagine yourself breathing in their condition or suffering. As you do this, imagine that you are breathing in their pain so you remove it from their bodies, giving them room for comfort, healing, and positivity.

Breathe out. As you breathe out, breathe happiness and peace out into the world. Think about what you think would bring them comfort or joy. Focus on that, and breathe it out into the world. Imagine that breath traveling to those you want to help, and having it fill that empty space with what they need.

Repeat. Continue this practice of breathing in pain and breathing out peace, over and over again, until your session is over. Remember, this does not just apply to others either. If you are in pain, you can breathe in and out your own suffering.

# Chapter 6

# The Ten Perfections (Parami, Pali; Paramita, Sanskrit)

In Buddhism, there are various lists of perfections or qualities, that need to be practiced diligently. They all cover similar things, but the following list of 10 Paramis (perfections) comes from the Theravadan school. They are presented several times scattered in the Jataka tales as well as the Sutta Pitaka of the Pali Tipitaka. They are not listed together as a menu but are taught at various places in the suttas. They were, however, listed together very early on in Theravadan Buddhism.

That is listed in a deliberate order, one quality leading to the next. They are a complete set of practices, which help you rethink the Eightfold Noble Path, by looking at it from a different angle. These Paramis or cultivation of character can give you a new frame of reference to study the path. In any event, whether you study them separately or not, they need to be cultivated fully to reach awakening. They form an integral part of the Eightfold Noble Path.

# The Ten Paramis

1. Generosity   Dana
2. Morality     Sila
3. Renunciation  Nekkhama
4. Wisdom   Panna
5. Energy     Virya
6. Patience   Khanti
7. Truthfulness  Sacca
8. Determination   Adhitthana
9. Loving Kindness   Metta
10. Equanimity   Upekkha

## 1. Generosity –Dana

This is most available to everyone, even small children. This is a core teaching in all traditions and all other religions. It inspires and uplifts people, and causes them to emulate generosity. It is not just the act of giving, it needs the spirit and heart of generosity. Generosity results in joy for the giver. In giving we receive.

Being miserly and getting attached to accumulation and hoarding will lead to unhappiness and a feeling of lack. It fosters greed and avarice and can permeate out into society, resulting in ambition and conflict. This escalates into crime and wars. Generosity on the other hand fosters peace and harmony and it is infectious.

Lack of generosity in a family leads to resentment and conflict and a pathological family. The child will imitate the stinginess, and thus this way of life propagates into a society.

Generosity disarms people. It astonishes them and can be the start of a great transformation in someone. Generosity is the primary virtue, which acts as a base for all the other virtues. Without generosity, we could not label a person either wise or virtuous. It is a skill that can be learned. Before giving, learn to infuse it with joy. The value of generosity depends on your right intention not on how the receiver reacts to your generosity. The benefit is yours and the law of karma will return it to you with the same emotional conditions that you put into the giving.

Generosity requires skill and what you give should be appropriate. Do not give a Buddhist monk a bottle of whiskey for example. Listen to people and you will develop this skill. The timing of the giving is important and should be appropriate.

Gifts should be clean and given with respect, and with a virtuous heart. Also, the karmic return is greater when generosity is directed at people with high moral character. It is a fact that the reason that society does not completely fall apart is due to the people of high moral development. Generosity fosters the next perfection, which is morality or virtue.

### 2. **Morality  Sila**

Although it is said that moral behaviour flows naturally from releasing selfish desire, it is also the case that releasing selfish desire flows naturally from moral behaviour. This overlaps with the Eightfold Path which consists of Sila (morality) Samadhi (concentration ) and Panna (wisdom). We find the same sila showing up in the 10 paramis.

Morality has to be developed. We have already discussed the morality factors of the Eightfold Path, right speech, right action, and right livelihood. In this path, unless we develop a morality first, we cannot achieve samadhi which is right concentration. We cannot hope to make our mind lucid, still, and transparent, which in turn allows the arising of wisdom. Virtuous behaviour is essential in the path to the end of suffering. If you are striving for peace and clarity, in your life, moral behaviour is an essential ingredient.

Moral behaviour is also outlined in five precepts. This is not a relative teaching, it is an absolute teaching.

## The Five Precepts
1. To not kill living beings
2. To not take what is not given
3. To not act sexually in a harmful way
4. To not lie, use harsh words, or gossip
5. To not partake of intoxicants which lead to further confusion

Appreciation of giving, and living in harmony with others, leads to the next perfection of renunciation.

## 3. Renunciation Nekkhamma
Renunciation, in Buddhism, can be understood as letting go of whatever binds us to suffering and ignorance. This is a subtle skill because those things that bind us, are the very things we mistakenly think we must have to be happy.

The Buddha taught that genuine renunciation requires thoroughly perceiving how we make ourselves unhappy by being ignorant of the cause which is desire and aversion. When we developed this wisdom renunciation naturally follows, and it is a positive and liberating act, not a punishment.

Monastics renounce the household life and all that goes with it. The Buddha said work and families can be a dirty narrow life whereas monastic life is spacious and imbued with freedom. Power, wealth, and fame is what most people of the world aspire to, but they can be a roadblock to awakening. Renunciation is unburdening of the demands that life makes. If you contemplate death, you will see that everyday life is trivial. When somebody enters monastic life they see this truth, and they give up everything but the basics, which are shelter, food, clothing, and medicine which are prerequisites of human survival.

Shelter, when and what they eat, and how you get food are all restricted when you become a monk. No one would give up sensory pleasures and entertainment unless it was replaced with something better. Even medicine is restricted to monks. If you don't have money and your access to modern medicine is limited, it is a risk, but a risk that the monastic community feels is worth it.

The lifting of the burden and finding peace and joy and the end of suffering is so good that they are willing to give up everything.

In lay life, people can practice renunciation within their own reality. Some examples are:
Renounce erotica and limit sexual activity, and fantasy of sexual activity, for periods.
Stop surfing the Internet and replace this with meditation practice and studying Dharma.

3. Moderate intake of food and frequency of eating. Eat mindfully, and select healthy food and practice intermittent fasting.

Refrain from dependence on stylish, sexy clothes or exotic makeup.

Sleep on the floor, instead of in a soft bed.

Reduce the length of sleep, and perform more sitting and walking meditation and reflection. Deep relaxation meditation often reduces the requirement for sleep.

Once a month, spend most of the night meditating. Bring mindfulness and acceptance to the discomfort felt.

Limit your clothing. When you buy a new shirt given the old one away.

Every time you indulge yourself, do it for another as well. For example, if you buy a coffee, give one to someone else as well. Every time you give something to yourself, also give something to another. Renunciation is said to be perfected by wisdom, which is the next perfection.

## 4. Wisdom Panna

There is an infinite number of questions, that humans could ask. There is an infinite amount of knowledge out there. Intelligent people are people who have a lot of knowledge and can answer questions. Intelligent people are not necessarily wise. Wisdom is having the insight to know what questions to ask. The Buddha tells us that the most important question is to ask how to end suffering. Therefore, wisdom is the knowledge and insight that you need, in the service of the end of suffering.

Wisdom is the crown jewel in the dharma and is the direct path to awakening and the end of suffering. Wisdom is the pivot around which all the other perfections revolve.

You cannot practice generosity, morality, or renunciation properly without wisdom. Buddhism differs from other religions, which teaches that there is no external agency that we can rely on to save us. We have to make the right effort and walk the right path, to gain the wisdom, that is required to end suffering. The advice of the Buddha or outside mentors is helpful, but each person has to walk the path themselves.

Wisdom requires a bedrock of morality. Mindfulness and Samma samadhi cause it to arise and swell. Without right view and right intention, this is impossible. The path starts with superficial wisdom and it ends with deepening and perfecting wisdom.

Wisdom is required to understand and penetrate the Four Noble Truths and Eightfold Noble Path. This will entail an understanding that ignorance causes the roots of suffering, which are desire and aversion. Wisdom requires that we grasp fully the universal truths of impermanence, no- self, and dukkha. Without wisdom, we cannot overcome the five hindrances. Without wisdom practicing loving-kindness, equanimity and all the other factors of enlightenment is not possible. Wisdom is required to ripen right view and right intention, and all the other elements of the path. Wisdom is required to understand the entire Dharma and put it into practice. We need to have a polygamous relationship with the 10 perfections and not serial marriages. That is to say, we need to practice the 10 perfections all at the same time and not one after the other.

Wisdom is perfected by the next parami—energy.

## 5. Energy Virya

Energy refers to walking the spiritual path with the fearlessness and determination of a warrior. It means following the path with diligence and steadfast interest, despite obstacles. Such fearlessness follows naturally from the perfection of wisdom.

Energy directed in the wrong direction can be problematic. Hitler, Stalin, and Napoleon all had plenty of energy, but without the wisdom of direction. Energy overcomes the hindrance of torpor.

Energy can be stirred up with urgency, by appreciating the uncertainty, brevity, and impermanence of life. This can be done through reflection and meditation. If someone walks into your room and points a gun at you, your energy surges, as you are brought face-to-face with the brevity and uncertainty of life.

Loving-kindness and joy foster energy. Living virtuously, and generously, generates energy. Courage infuses you with energy. Wisdom gives you energy as you solve problems. Borrowed wisdom, by receiving advice from others can energize you. Patience and equanimity foster energy. Reactivity to unpleasant events drains your energy and non-reaction retains energy. Energy spiderwebs out to every other parami. Energy is infectious and energizes other people. The perfection of channeling energy and effort helps bring about patience.

### 6. Patience Khanti
Having developed the energy and fearlessness of a warrior, patience gives us endurance, tolerance and composure, and the ability to withstand an onslaught. To

practice the parami of patience is to accept all that happens with equanimity, and understanding that whatever happens, it is a part of the spiritual path.

Patience helps us endure the hardships of our own lives, as well as the suffering created by others. Patience helps us to overcome problematic situations non-reactively. Patience rescues us from anger, which is one of the roots of suffering. Patience allows us to endure negative events without resentment, frustration, or anger. These things poison your body and your personality. In the Buddha's words, "patience closes off the doorway to the plane of misery."

When people attack you or are unpleasant towards you, see it as a spiritual lesson, see it as an opportunity to practice patience. There are ways to deal with these problems non-reactively and with no suffering on your part. Endurance implies that you are putting up with something but still suffering. True patience means you have found a way to respond without any suffering on your part.

## 7. Truthfulness Sacca

Nothing can be accomplished without truth. The understanding of the truth of the four noble truths and the dharma embodies truthfulness. Different truths have different values. Scientific truth is where we endeavour to prove a hypothesis, which then becomes a scientific truth. The Buddha is not preoccupied with that kind of truth. The Buddha is interested in the truth of suffering. We could call it right truth or truth in the service of enlightenment. The Buddha would advise truthfulness about all truths, including scientific truth, but that is not our focus here.

We need to tell ourselves the truths of existence, which are impermanence, insubstantiality,  and dukkha. Sometimes we forget that, and tell ourselves a lie, like something that we are attached to will last. It is vital that we start by telling the truth to ourselves and then to others. If we don't cultivate a general inquiry into the truth, suffering will ensue.

Wisdom and truth are inseparable. To be wise is to recognize the truth, and to recognize the truth is to be wise. The final stage of enlightenment is to recognize the truth of the Four Noble Truths. Truthfulness helps us develop the next parami, which is determination.

## 8. Determination  Adhittana

Determination is a resolve to continue along the path no matter what obstacles present themselves. It helps us clarify what is necessary for enlightenment and what is not.

None of the other paramis can be cultivated without determination and persistence. Success along the path is dependent on determination. Determination is vital for success in anything in life.

Determination can be artificially divided into three categories of things to be determined about.
Easy to do, say a 90% chance of success.
Moderately difficult to do, say a 50% chance of success
Difficult to do, say a is 10% chance of success
Even if we activate determination, and we fail, all is not lost. That failure is an important part of our path. Even if we fail, we still maintain patience and equanimity, and we

reset the determination. The determination to stay on a clear, unfettered path, helps develop loving-kindness.

## 9. Loving-kindness Metta

Loving-kindness is a mental state cultivated by practice. It involves a deliberate and total abandonment of self-centeredness, in favour of understanding that the suffering of others is our own suffering. Perfecting metta is essential to doing away with the self-clinging that binds us to suffering. Metta is the antidote to selfishness, anger, and fear.

Loving-kindness is directing love toward a being that is happy or not. Loving-kindness includes compassion, which is loving-kindness to people who are suffering. Loving-kindness includes sympathetic joy, which is loving-kindness towards joyful people.

True loving-kindness is unconditional and is like the rain, which is not concerned with where it falls. The radiation of loving-kindness is not always felt by the receiver, but the person who radiates loving-kindness always receives the benefits.

We can send loving-kindness even to our attackers and enemies because we know the cause of their behaviour is ultimately ignorance. They are ignorant of the fact that their behaviour leads to suffering for themselves, and others. As Jesus said, "Forgive them for they know not what they do"! We recognize that any being who is behaving unskilfully is suffering.

There are many benefits of loving-kindness. Here are some of them. You sleep and awake easily. You will have pleasant dreams. People will love and respect you. You will transform your subconscious mind. You, will less likely, be harmed by others. Your face will be radiant and your mind serene. You will die unconcerned and you will live a happy life.

# Chapter 7

# Enlightenment

Enlightenment is an English word, which has wildly different meanings for different people. Let us first look at what early Buddhist teachings taught, in the suttas, about the stages of enlightenment. This teaching still survives in the Theravadan tradition of Buddhism today.

The path to enlightenment, they say, is first the Eightfold Noble Path, which starts with limited initial wisdom, progresses to ethical purification, and then to a combination of right effort, mindfulness and concentration, which then turns back to penetrate wisdom fully, which is the direct forerunner of enlightenment. They particularly emphasize that insight into anatta (no-self) is the forerunner to liberation. The oldest Buddhist texts, portray the Buddha as referring to people who are at one of four stages of enlightenment.

Sotapanna –stream-enterer
Sakadagamin—a once-returner
Anagani—a non-returner
Arahant—a fully enlightened being

There is some argument about whether these stages are reached gradually or each one suddenly happens in a moment after a period of preparation. Whether it happens in four distinct moments or where that is a gradual thing, the result is the same. An Arahant is at the same level of enlightenment as a Buddha. The difference is an Arahant gets there by following the teachings of a Buddha. A Buddha gets enlightened directly by his efforts and his own path.


**Sotapanna**—stream-enterer: this means one has left the normal life, to enter the stream of supernormal life as outlined by the Dharma. The Sotapanna has an intuitive grasp of the three characteristics of the Dharma, impermanence, unsatisfactoriness, and no-self, which is empty of inherent existence. Theravadan's say that the final Arahantship will be reached in a maximum of seven lifetimes.

It is attainable by laypeople and monastics alike, and in the time of the Buddha, there were many thousands of people who reach this state. The core requirement is that it is a realization that alters who you are. You have a personality change, a transformation. You have a completely different view of reality. It deactivates some strong negative tendencies. Mostly anger and greed are markedly reduced, but not yet totally overcome. One is no longer able to kill or steal intentionally. The qualities of loving-kindness, compassion, sympathetic joy and equanimity are strongly developed.

The person is ethically transformed, but this is not merely a decision to follow ethical rules, it is a change of heart, which comes about by reflection on the three characteristics of impermanence, unsatisfactoriness, and no-self.

In various suttas, the Buddha gives various lists of factors that prevent enlightenment. Theravadans list 10 fetters and at this stage, the first three fetters fall away.

### The Ten Fetters

Self-identity
Skeptical doubt
Attachment to wrongful rites and ritual
Sensual desire
Ill will
Attachment to form realms
Attachment to formless realms
Conceit, arrogance or pride
Restlessness
Ignorance (of dharma)

Firstly, self-identity falls away and the person recognizes the emptiness of self.

Secondly, you have practiced the dharma and do not doubt that it is true. You have seen the truth for yourself and this second factor of doubt falls away. All doubt concerning the core teachings of the Dharma has fallen away.

Thirdly, you realize that liberation is only achieved by wisdom and introspection, not by rites or rituals. This factor is sometimes referred to as abandonment of rights and rituals, as a means to liberation.

Ethical behaviour lays the foundation for liberation, but it is not in itself a direct path. It is insight and wisdom, which is needed, for liberation. The first stage of enlightenment is irreversible. If it is reversible, you are not a stream-enterer. This Sotapanna can still live the household life and he may or may not have achieved the four Jhanas in meditation.

There are still slight remnants of anger and desire. They may still experience things like depression and the like, but it is markedly reduced. It is just a matter of time before total liberation is reached.

**Sahadagamin**—a once-returner: it was said, that there is a maximum of one human lifetime left before Arahantship. Anger and greed are weakened even further. You can remain in the household life. Under direct provocation, anger or desire might still arise.

**Anagami**—a non-returner. The non-returner does not return to the human world, or any unfortunate world lower than that. The fourth and fifth factors of anger and desire are overcome. It is still possible to remain in the household life, but usually, there is no more desire to live like that, and so you are essentially a monk in a household.

**Arahant**-- final liberation: the last five subtle fetters are overcome. These are attachment to the pleasures of Jhana or Arupa meditation, and any remnant of restlessness of the mind is overcome. The mind does not move around anymore. Restlessness of the mind is replaced with equanimity. Any vestiges of conceit about the sense of self are gone. Ignorance of the sense of self is fully overcome. There is no vestige of self left. All five subtle fetters of the Anagami are overcome. There are no further rebirths into any realm of existence. There is no more kharma and Nirvana is attained.

Because of the fetter of attachment to Jhana states, some schools of Buddhism warn you against doing Jhana meditation. This is strange advice because you only get to release this fetter at the final stage, and Jhanic meditation is a big help on the path that you need to follow. The Buddha outlined its use to achieve right concentration, through right effort and right mindfulness, which then leads to the wisdom and insight that you need to enter the stream. When you are one step away from Arahantship, you can address this attachment, not before.

Mahayana and Vajrayana (Tibetan) Buddhism come at it from a different perspective. They say that the goal should be to become a bodhisattva, which is a person who strives for enlightenment but vows to stay in samsara to teach as many people as possible about enlightenment. They emphasize compassion and wisdom and teach that one is striving for enlightenment for all beings, not just themselves. They call this the Greater Vehicle, and the personal enlightenment route they call the Lesser Vehicle. They say the Buddha lived more than 500 lives like this before circumstances were right for Nirvana and we should do the same. Nirvana is the end of suffering, the end of karma, and no more rebirths into samsara.

### Enlightenment and Universal Truth
Enlightenment is not something you can make a goal to achieve. I have made a million dollars, that didn't satisfy me. I married a beautiful woman, that was unsatisfactory. Perhaps enlightenment will satisfy me? Let me find out

what it is, and pursue that as a goal. That will not work. That is just the ego pursuing another concept. Enlightenment is the egoless state, so while you are asking that question, that's not it.

Better motivation would be to seek liberation from suffering. Ask yourself, "What do I need to do to end my suffering, and experience peace of mind?" You will discover, that no circumstances external to you will achieve that permanently. Everything external to you, all phenomena, are impermanent. You will come to realize that even you are impermanent, and there is no permanent self. In Buddhism we call this emptiness, other religions might call this God. Until you experience this oneness with God, or emptiness, by penetrating this understanding, suffering will continue. Sometimes this is called non-duality, God-realisation, self-realization, awakening, finding the Kingdom of Heaven.

Whatever words you want to use to describe it, this egoless state, which has no desires or aversion is where you need to get to, to arrive at the end of suffering. It requires wisdom to get there and it will result in you becoming filled with loving-kindness, compassion, sympathetic joy, and equanimity. It is living in this state all of the time, which shows that you have been liberated from suffering, and which means you live in a state of peace and joy. You will live an abundant life. It means that you have found the Kingdom of Heaven, which is within.

Is there only one path to this state? Is there no other way, other than through the Buddha's dharma? Whether you get there via the Buddha, Jesus, the Upanishads, Islam, or other spiritual paths, it is all the same state. There are many paths to the top of the mountain. These paths cannot be adequately described in words. You need to seek and find the path yourself, by using the pointers left by true spiritual teachers, of which the Buddha is a remarkable one. The Buddha has left us with clear, step by step instructions, on how to get there. He leads us through the basics, building our wisdom clearly and gradually. Follow the dharma diligently and put it into practice and the end of suffering, which is peace and joy, will be yours!

There is an enormous amount of Buddhist literature out there. I have tried to stick to the essential basics of the original teachings of the Buddha. This is embraced by the Theravadan tradition and is a good place to start. Use this little book as a springboard to start out in Buddhism. Only by putting the teachings into practice, will they benefit you. This is also the only way that you will test the teachings and know for yourself that they are true.

# Appendix

## Glossary

| Pali | Sanskrit | English |
|---|---|---|
| Adhittana | | Determination |
| Anagani | | Non-returner |
| Anatta | | No-self |
| Anicca | | Impermanence |
| Arahant | | Fully enlightened |
| Arupa | | Formless |
| Bodhisattva | | Enlightenment striver |
| Brahmins | | Priests of highest castes |
| Buddha | | Awakened one |
| Citta | | Mind states |
| Dana | | Generosity |
| Dhamma | Dharma | Teachings of Buddha |
| Dukkha | Duhkha | Suffering |
| Ekagghata | | Oneness, immersion |
| Jhana | | Stillness meditation |
| Kamma | Karma | Action and consequences |
| Karuna | | Compassion |

| Kaya | | The body |
| Khanti | | Patience |
| Mahayana | | Great vehicle |
| Metta | | Loving-kindness |
| Mudita | | Sympathetic joy |
| Nekkhama | | Renunciation |
| Nibbana | Nirvana | End of suffering & samsara |
| Panna | | Wisdom |
| Parami | Paramita | Perfections |
| Piti | | Glee or bodily pleasure |
| Rupa | | Form or object |
| Sacca | | Truthfulness |
| Sakagamin | | Once-returner |
| Samadhi | | Concentration |
| Samma | | Right, in the service of |
| Sampapalapa | | Gossip, blah blah blah |
| Samsara | | Rebirths into dukkha |
| Sangha | Sanga | Buddhist community |
| Sila | | Moral discipline |
| Sotapanna | | Stream enterer |
| Sukha | | Happiness or joy |
| Sunyata | | No enduring thing |
| Sutta | Sutra | A teaching of Buddha |
| Theravada | | Doctine of the Elders |
| Tipitaka | Tripitaka | 3 Baskets of Pali canon |
| Uphekka | | Equanimity |
| Verdana | | Feelings or emotions |
| Viriya | | Energy |

# Buddhism Lists
## Lists of Three

### The Three Refuges (jewels)
Buddha
Dharma
Sanga

### The Three Universal truths
Anicca
Dukkha
Anatta

### The Three Divisions of Teachings
Sila (morality, virtue)
Samadhi (concentration)
Panna (wisdom)

### The Three Poisons (unwholesome roots of dukkha)
Desire
Aversion
Ignorance

## Lists of Four

### The Four Noble Truths
Dukkha Exists
Dukkha is caused by craving
Stop craving and dukkha stops
How? The Eightfold Noble Path

### The Four Foundations of Mindfulness
The Physical Body
Initial reaction to sensory input
Mind states, moods
Dharma teachings

### The Four Highest emotions
Metta loving kindness
Karuna compassion
Mudita sympathetic joy
Upekkha equanimity

### Lists of Five

### The Five Precepts
To not kill living beings
To not take what is not given
To not act sexually in a harmful way
To not lie, slander, use harsh words, or gossip
To not take intoxicants, that leads to confusion

### The Five Hindrances
Sensual desire
Anger or ill will
Sloth or torpor
Restlessness
Skeptical doubt

**The Five dharmas to practice mindfulness**
The Five Hindrances
The Seven factors of awakening
The Five khandas (see below)
The Six senses and fetters they generate
The Four Noble truths

**The Five Khandas (Heaps or aggregates)**
Rupa-- physical form
Vedana-- initial reactions to sensory input
Sanna-- perception, identifying the ability of the mind
Sankhara-- thoughts, emotions, and memories
Vennana-- consciousness

**The Five Faculties (or Strengths)**
Faith
Energy
Mindfulness
Concentration
Wisdom

**List of Six**

**The Six Senses**
Seeing
Hearing
Smelling
Tasting
Touching
Thinking

**List of Seven**

**The Seven Factors of Enlightenment**
Mindfulness
Investigation of dharma
Energy
Rapture (piti)
Tranquility
Concentration
Equanimity


**Lists of Eight**

**Noble  Eightfold Path**
Right View
Right Intention
Right Speech
Right Action
Right Livelihood
Right Effort
Right Mindfulness
Right Concentration

**Eight Worldly Conditions**
Praise
Blame
Loss
Gain/Pleasure
Pain
Fame
Ill-fame

# List of Ten

## The Ten Perfections
Generosity
Morality
Renunciation
Wisdom
Energy
Patience
Truthfulness
Determination
Loving Kindness
Equanimity

# Re-incarnation or rebirths—a personal view

Many people have a problem with grasping multiple rebirths into different bodies. My personal view resonates with what "A Course in Miracles" says about the matter, which goes as follows.

In the ultimate sense, reincarnation is impossible. We do not exist in duality, we are all part of the same creation which is eternal. There is no past or future, there is only the present moment. The question should be "Is the concept helpful?"; and it is a concept, and all concepts are empty. If it is used to strengthen the recognition of the eternal nature of existence, it is helpful indeed. If one is not careful it can be detrimental, as misuse offers preoccupation and perhaps pride in the past. It can induce inertia in the present.

If you dwell on this concept as a problem in the future, the task at hand is to escape from that problem now. If you are laying the groundwork for future life, you can only work out your liberation now. If someone is comforted by the concept of reincarnation, and it heartens them, the value is self-evident.

I am certain that liberation from suffering can be achieved by those who believe in reincarnation, and by those who do not. I believe that belief in the concept is not essential for awakening, which happens in the now. There is a risk in seeing the present in terms of the past, but it is good in any thought that strengthens the idea that life and the body are not the same. This is the essential truth found in anicca (no-self).

A teacher should be as helpful to those who believe in it, as well as to those who do not. It should not become a stumbling block, and I believe that there is no benefit in taking a definite stand. I feel that the Buddha used it as a teaching aid to point to an aspect of universal truth, that cannot be put in words. This is a personal view, and in no way reflects any official teaching of any school in Buddhism.

www.ingramcontent.com/pod-product-compliance
Lightning Source LLC
Chambersburg PA
CBHW031150130726
47988CB00006B/2619